Dedicated to
American Friends
Who Fought Heroically in China Battlefield
of World's Anti-Fascist War

献给
在世界反法西斯战争中国战场上
英勇战斗的美国朋友

Chief Advisor: Zhao Qizheng
Chief Director: Li Bing
Editorial Director: Guo Changjian
Chief Editor: Li Xiangping
Deputy Chief Editors: Wu Wei Lei Jia

Text: Ma Yufu
English Translators: Ma Baoxin Jiang Xuehong Sun Changcun Zhang Zudui Li Bo
English Advisors: Yu Fuxiang Meng Genfu
Editor: Li Dongwei
Executive Editor: Tang Hewei
Advisors: Geng Chengkuan Zhou Xiaoning

Design: Zhang Jianhua
Layout: Yan Zhijie
Art Editor: Yan Zhijie Liu Na Yang Jiansheng

总 顾 问：赵启正
总 策 划：李 冰
主　　编：郭长建
总 编 辑：李向平
副 主 编：吴 伟 雷 珈

撰　　稿：马毓福
英文翻译：马保新 蒋学宏 孙长存 张组对 李 博
英文审校：俞福祥 孟根福
编　　辑：李东卫
责任编辑：汤贺伟
军史顾问：耿成宽 周小宁

装帧策划：张建华
装帧设计：闫志杰
版式设计：闫志杰 刘 娜 杨建生

Col. C. L. Chennault and Flying Tigers

陈纳德和飞虎队

Masterminded by

the State Council Information Office of the People's Republic of China

策划

中华人民共和国国务院新闻办公室

Published by China Intercontinental Press

五洲传播出版社

C O N T

American Volunteer Group

The 23rd Fighter Group of 10th Air Force

The 14th Air Force of U.S. Army

E N T S

Claire Chennault was a famous USAF general during the World War II. In 1937, Claire Chennault came to China by request of Song Meiling (wife of Chian Kai-shek). He worked as an advisor and participated in the air combat in the initial Anti-Japanese War. In Nov. 1940, he returned to U.S. to recruit American air volunteers to come to China for war. In August, 1941, China and U.S. governments permitted to found The American Volunteer Group (AVG), better known as Flying Tigers, under the command of Claire Chennault, who successively held the posts of commander of 23rd Fighter Group of U.S. Army 10th Air Force (American Air Task Force in China), brigadier general, and commander of U.S. Army 14th Air Force, major general. The airpower under the leadership of Claire Chennault gave a heavy blow to the Japanese aggressors, especially the Japanese Air Force (JAF) (Japan had no independent Air Force at that time, here the JAF refers to Japanese Army Air Force and Navy Air Force) and achieved glorious victory. The Flying Tigers gained considerable fame for a time and Claire Chennault became a legendary hero.

陈纳德是第二次世界大战期间的著名美国空军将领。1937 年，陈纳德应宋美龄邀请，来中国任航空委员会顾问，并参加了抗日战争初期的对日本飞机空战。1940 年 11 月，他回美国招募航空志愿人员来中国作战。经中美两国政府批准，次年 8 月，建立“美国志愿航空队”即“飞虎队”，陈纳德任指挥官。以后他历任美国陆军第十航空队第 23 战斗机大队（“美国驻华空军特遣队”）准将指挥官、美国陆军第十四航空队少将司令官等职。这支由陈纳德领导、指挥的空中力量，从空中给日本侵略军，特别是日本空军（抗日战争期间日本无独立空军，只有陆军航空队和海军航空队。这里所指的日本空军，即日本陆军航空队和海军航空队）以沉重打击，并取得辉煌战绩，“飞虎队”名噪一时，陈纳德也成为传奇式的英雄人物。

Col. C. L. Chennault

I
美国志愿航空队

American Volunteer Group

1-1

The Founder and Commander of Flying Tigers, Claire Chennault

“飞虎队”的创始人和指挥官陈纳德

Claire L. Chennault was born in Commerce, Texas, on September 6, 1890. His father farmed cotton. In his early years, Chennault matriculated at Louisiana State University, specializing in agriculture and then studied in the State Normal School. After graduation, he worked as a headmaster of a primary school. And he got married soon. In 1917, he was drafted into army and received military training in a military academy in Indiana, and then working as signalman. Later, he became an officer and received lieutenant's bars when the World War I ended. The role of aircraft in war attracted military world's high attention and every nation was developing aviation, especially military aviation. Chennault who loved flying and dedicated himself to aviation took advantage of his good relations with some flight instructor to study bootleg flying lessons. After a period of study, he mastered the skill of how to fly the plane, "Jonny". At that time, every nation was laying emphasis on the development of military aviation and aviators were in urgent need. Because of his mastery of basic flying technique, Chennault was assigned to the 46th fighter squadron of US Army Air Corps as a pilot, and then promoted to deputy commander of the squadron.

In August, 1921, he received regular training and began to study and made research on the air combat tactics. Owning to his hard study and more skillful flight, Chennault became a superlative pilot, and in time he was assigned to Hawaii as commander of the 19th Fighter (Pursuit) Squadron. After analytical research on air combat tactics, Chennault thought that the air combat tactics for single plane applied in World War I had insufficient combat capability and was vulnerable to

克莱尔·李·陈纳德 1890 年 9 月 6 日生于美国德克萨斯州的康麦斯，其父是以种植棉花为生的农民。陈纳德早年在路易斯安那州州立大学学习农业专业，后转入该州师范学院学习，毕业后在一所小学任校长，不久结婚。1917 年应征入伍，在印第安那州军事学校接受军事训练，任通信兵，后提升为军官，军衔晋至中尉。这时第一次世界大战已经结束，飞机在战争中的作用引起军方的高度重视，各国都在发展航空事业，特别是军事航空。热爱飞行有志于航空事业的陈纳德，利用他与一些飞行教官熟识的条件，偷着学习飞行技术。他经过一段时间学习，掌握了驾驶“詹尼”飞机的飞行技术。当时各国都在竞相发展军事航空，招募航空人员，陈纳德由于掌握了基本飞行技术被调入美国陆军第 46 战斗机中队任飞行员，后升任该中队的副官。

1921 年 8 月他参加了正规飞行训练，并开始学习、研究第一次世界大战时的空战战术。由于陈纳德刻苦钻研，飞行技艺超群，1923 年被任命为驻夏威夷第 19 战斗机(当时称驱逐机）中队指挥官。通过对空战战术的分析研究，陈纳德认为第一次世界大战中使用的单机空战，因缺乏整体协调配合，战斗力不强，容易遭受对方攻击。他提出了双机和三机编队空战理论。陈纳德认为双机协同作战，僚机掩护长机进行攻击；长机可以集中精力攻击敌机，有利于提高命中率。同时，在僚机处于有利位置时，长机也可以掩护僚机进行攻击。陈纳德认为，采用 3 机编队战术，以 2 架飞机实施攻击，第 3 架飞机在高空掩护，可以胜过 6 架散开单独作战的飞机。

attack because they lacked integration and synchronization. He advanced the air combat theories of double-plane formation and triple-plane formation. He thought that coordinated two-ship attack was available. A wing plane could cover a lead plane in favorable attack position to make concentrated-attention attack on adversary planes, and vice versus, which contributed to the hit probability. In the triple-plane formation, two planes could engage in attack with the high-level cover of the third plane. Chennault thought that three planes could exceed 6 planes that were separated and fought individually after the application of the tactics of triple-plane formation.

In April, 1929, Claire Chennault was assigned to Brookes base as flight director, promoted to Captain. In order to verify the air combat theories of double-plane formation and triple-plane formation, Chennault organized trial flights. However, the pilots who had been used to the freedom of individual air combat was not accustomed to the strict formation combat, so the initial trial flight resulted in collision. His theory did not attract attention, and even worse, was mocked by some old pilots. Even then he was not downhearted but continued his research on tactics of air combat. He flew many formations for simulated air combat together with his comrades, other two pilots and achieved a better result. He read many books and materials, calculated various fight data, and finally wrote a new textbook of aerial combat tactics for combat teamwork of double-plane and triple-plane formations. He thought that the difference in the number of firepower of opposing sides was the square of the difference of fire weapons. Therefore, if a double-plane formation made a coordinated attack on a single adversary plane, the given superiority ratio is 4:1 instead of 2:1. Claire Chennault paid great attention to the importance of combat teamwork of double-plane and triple-plane formations. In order to perfect pilots' act in the air, he let three planes fly tied together with 65 meters lengths of control cable taking off, and landing with the tethers intact and it seemed as if the three planes were activated by a single mind. But Chennault's superiors regarded their performance as "Aerobatic Show" and didn't think the tactics of the formations would be effective in real war.

1929 年 4 月陈纳德被任命为布鲁克斯基地飞行主任，同时晋升为上尉。陈纳德为了验证双机和三机编队的空战理论，组织人员和飞机进行试飞，因飞行员们习惯于自由自在的单机空战，对严格编队空战非常不适，首次试飞就发生空中双机相撞事故，他的理论非但未能引起人们的注意，反而遭到一些守旧的老飞行员嘲笑。但他并没有因此而气馁，而是继续进行空战战术研究。他与 2 名志同道合飞行员进行多次编队飞行，模拟空战，并取得较好的效果。陈纳德阅读了大量图书资料，计算各种飞行数据，编写出新的双机、三机编队协同作战空战战术教材。他认为，在其他因素相同的条件下，敌对双方火力数量的差异是火器差异的平方。因此，两架飞机组成的编队，协同攻击一架单独的敌机，他们获得的优势不是二比一，而是四比一。陈纳德十分强调双机、三机编队协同作战的重要性。为了表现飞行员的熟练技巧，他用 65 米长的绳索分别将三架飞机连在一起，三架飞机在空中飞行就像一个人操纵一样，飞机着陆后，绳索仍保持原样。但是，陈纳德的上司把他们的表演认为是"耍杂技"，并不相信他的双机、三机编队战术会在实战中发挥作用。

Claire L. Chennault, the founder of American Volunteer Group (Flying Tigers), was a prestigious and competent commander.And his associates often called him "Oldman".
"美国志愿航空队"（"飞虎队"）的创始人克莱尔·李·陈纳德，是一个有威望、有能力的指挥官，人们习惯称他"老头子"。

On April 30, 1937, he retired from the U.S. Army Air Corps at age of 47. After his retirement, he lived in a country villa near Lake St. John in Waterproof, Louisiana and continued his research on aerial combat tactics for double-plane and triple-plane formations. His two assistants, Williamson and McDonald went to China as flight instructor after their retirement. When they were informed that Chinese Government intended to invite an air advisor for Aeronautical Commission (the highest authority of Chinese Air Force), they recommended Claire Chennault to the government and made many telephone calls to Chennault to persuade him to show his talent in China.

In June, 1937, Claire L. Chennault accepted the offer to work as an advisor to Aviation Commission in China. His primary mission was to help China to establish a combat-capable Air Force. After a survey, Chennault thought Chinese Air Force (CAF) lacked aircraft and the aircraft that could be used for real war were no more than 100, and some of them were war-vintage machines. Moreover, the CAF's airmen

1937 年 4 月 30 日，陈纳德从陆军航空队退役，当时 47 岁。他退役后住在路易斯安那州瓦特普鲁温圣约翰湖的乡间别墅，继续研究双机、三机编队空战战术。他的两位助手威廉·麦克唐纳和约翰·威廉姆森退役后去中国担任飞行教官，当他们得知中国政府要为“航空委员会”（当时中国空军的领导机关）聘请一位顾问时，就向中国政府推荐陈纳德。他们多次打电话给陈纳德，劝他到中国来展现他的才能。

1937 年 6 月陈纳德应聘到中国担任航空委员会顾问，其主要任务是帮助中国建设一支有战斗力的空军。陈纳德经过一番考察认为，中国空军飞机少，真正能够用于作战的飞机不足百架，而且有些是过时的飞机；飞行人员训练不足，特别是战术训练非常之差。由于航空技术装备不足和陈旧，一些飞行员在初级训练阶段就坠机丧生。他认为中国空军要发展就要添购性能先进的飞机，并加强飞行员的飞行技术、战术训练。

Claire Chennault (middle) having picture taken with his two assistants William McDonald (left) and John Williamson (right) in front of Boeing P-12E plane after the flight of double-plane and triple-plane formations.
陈纳德（中）与他的两位助手威廉·麦克唐纳（左）和约翰·威廉姆森进行双机、三机编队飞行后在波音 P-12E 飞机旁合影留念

In 1938, Claire Chennault talking with Italian advisor of CAF Officer School about the training condition of flying cadets.
1938 年陈纳德与在中国空军军官学校任职的意大利顾问交谈，了解飞行学员的训练情况。

lacked training, especially the tactical training. Just because of the shortage and the old of aircraft equipment, some pilots died of crash-land in initial training phase. Chennault thought that it was essential to import high-performance aircraft and strengthen the pilots' flight and tactical training for the development of CAF.

In July, 1937, the Anti-Japanese War broke out. The U.S. and U.K. did not want to export aircraft to China. CAF was forced into passive condition because of the non-replenishment of battle-damaged aircraft. The JAF (JAF) equipped with new type of aircraft gained prominent superiority. In the initial period of the war, the whole CAF was nearly drowned. Under that difficult condition, CAF received aids from Soviet Union and began to live up in every battlefield. After August, 1940, JAF began to bring in advanced aircraft Zero fighters. The USSR-made I-15, I-16 fighters used by CAF could not match the Zero fighters. The Japanese bombers, escorted by Zero fighters, often penetrated into the depth of China to make bombardment. China's major cities as Chongqing, Chengdu, Lanzhou, and some airbases often suffered JAF's attack. In June, 1941, Soviet-German war broke out. The USSR was unable to fend herself and could not provide aircraft to China. So, the Chinese Government could only depend on U. S. government for the support of a fighter unit and aircraft equipment to resist JAF. By that time, the relation between U. S. and Japan had become worse, which provided the Chinese government an opportunity to seek for aids from U.S.

1937 年 7 月抗日战争爆发后，美国和英国都不愿意把飞机卖给中国，中国空军因作战损失的飞机得不到补充而陷入被动，装备着新式飞机的日本空军占有明显优势。战争初期，中国空军几乎全军覆没。在中国空军最困难的时候，得到了苏联政府的援助，中国空军又活跃在各个战场。1940 年 8 月后，日本空军开始使用性能先进的“零”式战斗机，当时中国空军使用的苏制 I-15、I-16 战斗机不是“零”式战斗机的对手。日军轰炸机在“零”式战斗机的掩护下深入中国腹地轰炸，中国后方大城市重庆、成都、兰州等地及空军基地经常遭日本空军空袭。1941 年 6 月，苏德战争爆发后，苏联自顾不暇已无能力继续为中国提供飞机。中国政府寄希望于美国政府向中国提供一支战斗机部队和飞机装备，以抗击日本空军。这时日、美关系恶化，为中国政府谋求美国援助带来机会。

The main fighters used by CAF in August, 1940
1940年8月中国空军使用的主要战斗机

Polikarpov I-15 fighter: a single-seat plane made by Soviet Union National Aviation Industrial Company in 1934; length: 6.10m; wingspan: 9.75m; height 2.92m; powered with M25 air-cooled radial engine with 9 cylinders; horsepower: 700; overall weight: 1370kg; maximum speed: 368km/h; ceiling: 9800m; range: 500km; armament: 4 machineguns.

波里卡尔波夫 I-15 战斗机：乘员 1 人，1934 年苏联国家航空工业公司制造，机长 6.10 米、翼展 9.75 米、机高 2.92 米，装 700 马力 M-25 型 9 缸气冷星型发动机，全重 1370 千克，最大速度 368 千米/小时，升限 9800 米，航程 500 千米，武器 4 挺机枪。

Polikarpov I-16 fighter: a single-seat plane made by Soviet Union National Aviation Industrial Company in 1937: length: 6.07m; wingspan: 9.00m; height: 2.56m; powered with M25 air-cooled radial engine with 9 cylinders; horsepower: 775; overall weight: 2054kg; maximum speed: 464km/h; ceiling: 9000m; range: 800km; armament: 4 machineguns.

波里卡尔波夫 I-16 战斗机：乘员 1 人，1937 年苏联国家航空工业公司制造，机长 6.07 米、翼展 9.00 米、机高 2.56 米，装 775 马力 M-25B 型 9 缸气冷星型发动机，全重 2054 千克，最大速度 464 千米/小时，升限 9000 米，航程 800 千米，武器 4 挺机枪。

Main fighters used by Japanese aggressors in August, 1940

1940年8月侵华日军使用的主要战斗机

"Type 97" Nakajima Ki-27b land-based fighter: single-seat plane made by Japan Nakajima Plane Company in 1939; length: 7.53m; wingspan: 11.31m; height: 3.25m; powered with Nakajima air-cooled engine with 9 cylinders; horsepower: 710; overall weight: 1790kg; maximum speed: 470km/h; ceiling: 12365m; range: 1710km; armament: two 7.7mm-caliber machineguns, 100kg bombs.

97 式/中岛 Ki-27b 陆上战斗机：乘员 1 人，1939 年日本中岛飞机公司制造，机长 7.53 米、翼展 11.31 米、机高 3.25 米，装 710 马力中岛 Ha-1b 型 9 缸气冷星型发动机，全重 1790 千克，最大速度 470 千米/小时，升限 12365 米，航程 1710 千米，武器 2 挺 7.7 毫米机枪、100 千克炸弹。

Mitsubishi A5M4 fighter: a single-seat plane made by Japan Mitsubishi Industrial Company in 1939; length: 7.56m; wingspan: 11.00m; height: 3.27m; powered with Nakajima air-cooled engine with 9 cylinders; horsepower: 785; overall weight: 1671kg; maximum speed: 434km/h; ceiling: 9800m; range: 1200km; armament: two 7.7mm-caliber machineguns, 60kg bombs.

三菱 A5M4 战斗机：乘员 1 人，1939 年日本三菱重工业公司制造，机长 7.56 米、翼展 11.00 米、机高 3.27 米，装 785 马力中岛"寿"41 型 9 缸气冷星型发动机，全重 1671 千克，最大速度 434 千米/小时，升限 9800 米，航程 1200 千米，武器 2 挺 7.7 毫米机枪、60 千克炸弹。

Japan's Zero fighter is one of the famous fighters in World War II. Zero means the founding of an empire, and the year 2600 stands for 1940. The principal designer of A6M2 Zero fighter was Orikoshiziron. His plane is characteristic of high speed (maximum speed: 534km/h), high ceiling (10,000m), and strong firepower (two 7.7mm-caliber machineguns and the reformed one is equipped with two 20mm-caliber cannons). The plane also has its weakness. In order to reduce weight, the thin armor plate is used, so its structure is not of sufficient strength to withstand an attack. Diving performance is bad. The speed of steep and long-time dive cannot be over 660km/hour; otherwise the trembles can make the wings broken. The protection plate is too thin to protect their pilots. The oil tank, not the type of self-sealing fuel tank, is apt to catch fire once being hit. The instrument and electric devices are of poor quality and prone to accidents.

日本"零"式战斗机是第二次世界大战中杰出的战斗机之一。"零"是日本纪元 2600(1940)年纪元之意。A6M2"零"式战斗机主设计师堀越二郎。该机具有速度快(最大速度 534 千米/小时)，升限高(10000 米)，火力强，2 挺 7.7 毫米机枪(改进型装 2 门 20 毫米机炮)。"零"式战斗机的弱点是，为求重量轻金属蒙皮薄，因而结构不强，不耐打击；俯冲性能差，大角度与长时间俯冲，速度不能超过 660 千米/小时，否则，抖震会造成机翼折断；对飞行员的保护差，防护钢板很薄，无自封油箱，击中易着火；仪器、电气设备质量粗糙，容易出故障。

Mitsubishi A6M2 Zero fighter: a single-seat plane made by Japan Mitsubishi Industrial Company in 1940; length: 9.15m; wingspan: 12.10m; height: 3.05m; powered with Nakajima NK1C air-cooled engine with 9 cylinders; horsepower: 950; overall weight: 2800kg; maximum speed: 534km/h; ceiling: 10,000m; range: 3105km; armament: two 7.7mm-caliber machineguns, 120kg bombs.

三菱 A6M2“零”式战斗机：乘员 1 人，1940 年日本三菱重工业公司制造，机长 9.15 米、翼展 12.10 米、机高 3.05 米，装 950 马力中岛 NK1C“荣” 12 型 14 缸气冷星型发动机，全重 2800 千克，最大速度 534 千米/小时，升限 10000 米，航程 3105 千米，武器 2 挺 7.7 毫米机枪、120 千克炸弹。

In November, 1940, Chennault and Mao Bangchu, member of Aviation Commission, left for the United States, seeking to purchase a batch of combat aircraft and recruit some pilots. Chennault met all circles of Americans and explained the arduousness and importance of the Chinese War of Resistance against Japanese Aggression. After many twists and turns, Chennault's request that the United States help China's war efforts eventually won the support from Secretary of the Treasury Henry Morganthau and Deputy Secretary of the Navy for aviation Thomas Kirkland, and convinced President Roosevelt. On March 11, 1941, President Roosevelt signed the Lend Lease Act. According to the act, military equipment, such as fighter aircraft, could be lent or leased as rental material to China or any other countries. On April 15 of the same year, President Roosevelt also subscribed a confidential order that permit retired service personnel of U.S. Army and Navy, and the personnel of reserve forces to join American Volunteer Group. U.S. government provided China with 100 P-40B fighters that were manufactured for Great Britain, who would be refurnished with more advanced aircraft. In the name of Central Aircraft Manufacturing Company (CAMCO), Chennault and Song Ziwen (T. V. Soong), Chiang Kai-shek's private representative, recruited both air and ground crews from various places of the United States. They offered the following terms: the salary per month would be 600 dollars for pilots, 750 dollars for flight leaders, 350-400 dollars for aircraft maintenance people; there would be a 30-day paid leave for each person every year, and an allowance of 30 dollars each month. Later, Song Ziwen added a $500-bonus for every Japanese plane destroyed . Every member of AVG was obliged to sign as the volunteer member of Chinese Air Force (CAF), who would serve CAF and would be protected by international laws as prisoner of war among belligerents.

1940 年 11 月，陈纳德和航空委员会委员毛邦初从中国去美国，谋求得到一批作战飞机并招募一批飞行人员。陈纳德向美国各界人士介绍了中国抗战的艰巨性和重要性。几经周折，陈纳德关于要美国支持中国抗战的建议终于得到财政部长亨利·摩根索和海军部负责航空事务的次长托马斯·科克兰的支持，并说服了美国总统罗斯福。1941 年 3 月 11 日，罗斯福总统签署了“租借法案”，按照这项法案战斗机等武器装备可以作为租借物资出租给中国或其他国家。同年 4 月 15 日罗斯福总统又签署了一项密令，允许美国陆、海军退役军人及预备役军人参加美国志愿队前往中国。美国政府向中国提供了原先为英国生产的 100 架 P-40B 战斗机，以后以更先进的飞机补偿英国。陈纳德与蒋介石的私人代表宋子文以“中央飞机制造公司”的名义在美国各地招募空地勤人员，其条件是：每人每月工资，飞行员 600 美元，队长 750 美元；机械人员 350~400 美元，每年 30 天带薪金休假，外加每月 30 美元生活津贴。随后，宋子文又规定飞行员每击落一架日本飞机奖给 500 美元。每个志愿人员都必须签约作为中国空军志愿人员，为中国空军服务，并受到交战国被俘人员的国际保护。

1-2

Pre-War Training

战前训练

Among the recruited personnel, most aircrew members were retired bomber and transport pilots of Army Aviation, and only a minority of the aircrew members were retired fighter aircraft pilots. The ground crew members were also retired armed forces personnel and some of them were even civilians. Only with strict military and professional training could they be sent into real battle. To facilitate the training of the recruited air crews, Chennault needed a safe and cement-paved airfield that was out of the reach of Japanese aircraft. After a series of twists and turns, the British agreed to lend Chennault the Royal Air Force Keydaw airdrome, which was located in a forest of Toungoo, a town 274 kilometers from Rangoon, the capital of Burma. The first contingent of the American Volunteer Group, composed of 100 pilots and 50 maintenance and logistics personnel arrived at Keydaw airdrome in July, 1941. Before long, the second contingent also arrived. Later, a shipment of 100 P-40B fighter aircraft left the United States.One 1 aircraft fell to the sea during the convoy and only 99 aircraft actually reached their destination.

Chennault believed that it was purely a matter of sending the under-trained pilots to death if letting them fight in the air with the well-trained Japanese pilots. He imposed fairly strict requirement on the flying training for any of AVG members.

The training for AVG members consisted of two stages. The first stage was rudimental training, including 72 hours for learning of theoretical courses and 60 hours for basic skill in

招募来的空勤员多数是退役的原美国陆军航空队轰炸机、运输机飞行员，少数是退役的战斗机飞行员；地勤人员也是退役军人，其中有些是非军人出身。他们必须经过严格的军事训练和专业训练，才能够投入战斗。为了便于对招募来的空地勤人员进行训练，陈纳德需要一个日本飞机无法到达比较安全、有水泥跑道的机场。几经周折，英国同意将修建在距离缅甸首都仰光274千米，位于同古镇一片丛林中的凯德机场租给陈纳德使用。1941年7月，由100名飞行员、50名机械人员和后勤人员组成的第一批美国志愿人员到达缅甸同古镇凯德机场。不久，第二批美国志愿人员也到达凯德机场。后来陆续从美国运来P-40B战斗机100架，在港口搬运过程中1架掉入海中，实际只运到99架。

陈纳德认为，让没有训练好的飞行员匆忙上阵，同训练有素日本飞行员作战，等于让他们去白白送死，所以对志愿队队员飞行训练的要求非常严格。

飞行人员的训练分为两个阶段，第一阶段飞行基础训练：飞行理论课程72小时，基本飞行驾驶术（起落航线、空域飞行、编队飞行、转场飞行）训练60小时；第二阶段战术训练：战术理论课程12小时，战斗科目（空中射击、空中投弹、单机格斗、双机攻击、三机攻击、8~16机编队飞行、紧急迫降）训练20小时。在队员们基本掌握P-40战斗机飞行

flying (such as traffic pattern flying, airspace flying, formation flying, and ferry flying). The second stage was tactical training, including 12 hours for the courses on tactical theory, and 20 hours for fighting subjects (air firing, air bombing, individual-aircraft dogfight, double-aircraft attack, triple-aircraft attack, 8 – 16 aircraft formation flight, and emergency forced landing). After the pilots had gained the rudiment skills in controlling the P-40, Chennault continued the tactical training on air-to-air combating. The method of double-plane and triple-plane formation for air combating, which he had researched and studied for years, could now play its active role. The tactical training for air-battle skills was mainly focused upon the formation flying with double fighters and triple fighters, the dogfight in the air, and various ways of air fighting; while the training of air-to-ground attack was accomplished by learning how to hit a fixed ground target or attack various targets on ground.

Chennault gave lectures on the air-combat tactics for AVG members by himself. As he said, although the Japanese pilots were well-trained and brave, they lacked the sense of flexibility and initiative. What they would do in air-battle was to follow deadly the pre-determined plan, no matter how the situation in the air battle was changing. A formation of bombers would be kept as long as possible until the last bomber in the formation

驾驶技术后，开始空战战术训练，陈纳德多年探索、研究的双机和三机编队协调同作战方法，现在派上了用场。空战战术训练主要是双机和三机编队训练，空中格斗及各种攻击方法；对地攻击主要是打地靶和对各种目标的攻击方法。

陈纳德亲自为志愿队队员讲授空战战术课。他说，日本飞行员训练有素，作战很勇敢，但缺乏灵活性和主动性，总是按照预定的战术计划投入战斗，而不管空战中发生什么变化，轰炸机编队在被全部击落前，会一直保持队形；战斗机会连续使用相同的战术，不管是否有效。日本空军严厉的空中纪律，造成的固定战术模式，利用日本飞行员战术上的弱点是可以战胜他们的。陈纳德要求志愿队队员在空战中要千方百计打乱敌人队形，一旦日本飞行员被迫背离了他们的战术，就会陷入困境。他强调必须以己之长，击敌之短。日军“零”式战斗机的长处是爬升快、盘旋灵活，如果在盘旋中与敌缠斗，日本飞机就会占优势；P-40 战斗机的长处是，它的速度比“零”式战斗机快，机体坚固，装有防护装甲和防弹玻璃。陈纳德为志愿队规定，要充分利用 P-40 战斗机速度快的优点，从高空俯冲攻击并尽快脱离，采取打游击的办法，打了就跑，然后再爬高再次攻击，避免与敌人单机格斗。他还不断告诫志愿队队员们，在空战中

During their training at Keydaw, AVG often sent people to buy fresh food at the town of Toungoo to cater the trainees.
在凯德基地训练的美国志愿航空队经常派人到同古镇采购新鲜食物，以搞好伙食保证训练。

In Keydaw airbase, AVG used bamboo and wood to build up a simple control tower, on which Chennault often provided commanding and instructing for the flight training.
美国志愿航空队在凯德基地用竹木塔建的简易指挥塔，陈纳德经常在简易指挥塔上指挥飞行训练。

was shot down, and the fighters would continuously apply the same tactic, no matter whether such tactic is effective or not. The absolute sense of discipline observation in the air, as well as the unalterable tactical pattern of the JAF turned out to be the fatal weakness that might possibly be taken advantage of by AVG in the fighting. Chennault demanded that AVG pilot try every possible means to break down the enemy' s order in formation, and the Japanese pilots would immediately run into trouble once they were forced to break away from the existing layout. He emphasized that one must learn to win by using his own advantages against the enemy's weakness. The benefits of the Japanese Zero fighter lied in quick climbing and flexible banking turn. Therefore, the Japanese aircraft would have an advantage in the fighting during banking turn. Compared with Zero fighter, a P-40 fighter had a faster airspeed; besides, it had a more solid frame structure and was equipped protective armature and bulletproof glass. Based on those considerations, Chennault drew up a method of fully using the fast speed of P-40 to make a diving attack and then making breakaway quickly. Such way was somewhat like a guerrilla fight, i.e., run away after attacking on the enemy plane, and then re-climb for another attack. Avoid a dogfight individually with the enemy. He constantly exhorted AVG pilots never try to attack the enemy aircraft individually, and explained that a group of 2 P-40s might defeat as many as 6 Japanese aircraft. His approach, which was based upon his study over the Japanese air-fight tactics and the Japanese aircraft equipment through years, was regarded as non-formal by other people; however, his guerrilla-like tactics for air fight won time and again. Through half year of training, his troop could essentially participated in the real air war.

绝对不要单独去进攻，因为2机一组的P-40可以胜过6架日机。陈纳德根据自己多年来对日本空军空战战术和飞机装备的研究创造的空战战术，在别人看来是一种非正规战术，然而采用这种空中游击战术在以后的空战中却屡屡获胜。经过近半年时间的训练，这支队伍基本上能够参加实战了。

The P-40s used for the training at Keydaw base were painted with the emblem used by U.S. Army Aviation prior to 1940.
在凯德基地进行训练的 P-40B 战斗机，喷有美国陆军航空队 1940 年以前使用的机徽。

In the Summer of 1941,the fuselage of P-14 figher was winched to the position of fitting the Wing in Rangon,Burma. Left side shows the unfinished hangar.
1941 年夏天，缅甸仰光，正在绞起 P-14 机身就位，以便安装机翼。左为尚未完工的机库。

1-3

The Founding of American Volunteer Group

成立美国志愿航空队

On August 1, 1941, American Volunteer Group was founded at Keydaw airbase nearby Toungoo Town. Col. Chennault (ranked by Chinese Air Force) was appointed the leader for AVG. AVG consisted of three squadrons, with the first squadron led by Robert Sandell, the second by Jack Newkirk and the third by Arweide Olson. Each squadron was equipped with 18 P-40B/C fighters, in addition, there were another 10 for stand-by. In AVG, there were A/E technicians, armament technicians, radio operators, parachute riggers, chefs, bakers, cameramen, quartermasters, secretaries, weather servicemen, doctors, nurses and 1 accompanying clergyman, plus other service men sent by Chinese Air Force, amounting to 240 persons in total (the establishment required 270).

Though invested by Chinese Government and registered as an establishment in Chinese Air Force system, AVG was an air unit that was equipped with American aircraft, composed of American volunteers, and commanded by American for independent operation. However, any major issue should be reported to and asked for instruction from the Aeronautical Commission (the highest leading body of Chinese Air Force). Through the training period, AVG pilots were able to operate P-40 skillfully, and their air firing also yielded in good results; therefore, this air unit was basically empowered with air-fight capability. The major tasks allocated by Chinese Air Force for AVG were: to ensure air defense for the airbase within Kunming area, assist in the air-defense combat for the important areas at the front, attack the Japanese troops on the Burma Road to ensure the transportation along the Burma Road.

1941年8月1日，美国志愿航空队在缅甸同古镇凯德机场成立，由陈纳德上校（由中国空军任命为上校）任队长，下辖三个战斗机中队，第1中队中队长罗伯特·桑德尔、第2中队中队长杰克·纽科克、第3中队中队长阿维德·奥尔逊，每个中队装备18架P-40B/C战斗机，还有10架备用机；志愿队有机械师、军械师、无线电员、叠伞员、厨师、面包师、摄影师、军需官、文书、气象员、医生、护士和1名随队牧师，加上中国空军派赴该队服务人员共计240人（编制为270人）。

美国志愿航空队是中国政府出资，编入中国空军序列，装备美国飞机，完全由美国志愿人员组成，由美国人指挥独立作战的航空部队。但重大事情必须请示、报告“航空委员会”（中国空军最高领导机关）。经过一段时间的训练，飞行员们已经能够熟练地驾驶P-40战斗机，空中射击成绩也不错，这支队伍基本具备了空中作战能力。中国空军给美国志愿队的主要任务是：担负昆明地区基地防空，支援前线重要地区防空作战，打击滇缅公路的日军，保障滇缅公路运输。

Of this P-40B Warhawk fighter, the wing was painted with sign of Chinese Air Force, and the fuselage was marked with serial number, indicating that this aircraft belonged to Chinese Air Force and was included in the equipment system of Chinese Air Force; the nose was drawn with shark eyes and teeth, and the fuselage was painted with a flying tiger, indicating that it was an aircraft used by AVG; an angel was drawn in front of the windshield, showing that it belonged to the second squadron of AVG; beside the cockpit, there were ten ensigns of Japan, indicating the pilot of this P-40 had shot down ten Japanese aircraft.

这架 P-40B“战鹰”战斗机，机翼上有中国空军机徽，机身有飞机编号，表示飞机为中国空军所有，飞机列入中国空军装备序列；机头绘有鲨鱼的眼睛和牙齿，机身有一只“飞虎”，可以知道是美国志愿航空队使用的飞机；飞机风挡前机身画有“天使”，表示是第 2 中队的飞机；驾驶舱旁有 10 面日本小军旗，表示该机飞行员曾经击落过 10 架日本飞机。

P-40 was developed by American Curtiss Aircraft Company Inc.. In 1938, it made its virgin flight and was put into batch production in 1940. From Feb. 1942, it began to serve in American Army Air Force; later, it was supplied to Great Britain, the Soviet Union and China. The exported P-40 was typed as Hawk-81A. At beginning, P-40B/C fighters were equipped for AVG; and later, modified P-40E/K/N began to serve in AVG. Totally, there had been 13,000 P-40 fighters of various types being produced. The features of the P-40 include: solid structure for attack resistance; good protection for the pilot, with thick bulletproof glass installed behind the windshield, and steel plate and bulletproof self-sealing fuel tank behind the seat; strong firing power, with 4 - 6 12.7mm-calibre machineguns installed, enabling long-range shooting and cross firing, and working reliably. Though unsatisfactory in level flying and climbing, P-40 was good at diving; even in a vertical diving, it still had good controllability without any shivering. AVG members were enlightened by a picture of shark printed in an Indian pictorial; then they took the same way as what the Great Britain's Royal Air Force did in Africa to paint a pair of fierce eyes and two rows of big white teeth of shark on the cowling of the engine, to make the nose of P-40 alike the head of a tiger shark. It was said that the painting of shark eyes and teeth at the nose of P-40 had to certain extent threatened and scared the enemy.

P-40 由美国寇蒂斯飞机公司研制，1938 年 10 月首飞，1940 年批量生产，1941 年 2 月开始装备美国陆军航空队，后曾向英国、苏联、中国提供。出口型称“霍克-81A”。美国志愿航空队开始装备 P-40B/C 战斗机，后来又装备改进型 P-40E/K/N 战斗机。P-40 各型共生产 13000 多架，其特点是结实，能够承受打击；对飞行员保护性能好，风挡后有很厚的防弹玻璃，飞行员座椅后有钢板及防弹自封油箱；火力强，有 4~6 挺 12.7 毫米机枪，射程远、交叉火力强，工作可靠，极少发生故障。P-40 平飞和上升性能都不理想，但俯冲性能还好，即便作垂直俯冲，也不会产生抖震，操纵性能好。志愿队队员看了印度画报上的鲨鱼受到启发，并借用英国皇家空军在非洲的做法，在发动机外罩上绘了一付凶恶的眼睛和一排雪白的大牙齿，把突出的机头变成虎鲨的头部。美国志愿航空队的飞机机头都画上鲨鱼的眼睛和牙齿，据说可以震慑敌人。

P-40B Warhawk fighter: a single-seat plane made by American Curtiss Leiter Company in 1941; length: 9.68m, wing span: 11.38m, height: 3.23m; powered with Eilison V1710-33 type, 12-cylinder liquid cooled engine of 1,040 horse power; total weight: 3,450kg; max. speed: 566km/hr; ceiling: 9,875m; range: 1,500km; airborne weapon: one 12.7mm cannon.

P-40B“战鹰”战斗机：乘员 1 人，1941 年美国寇蒂斯·莱特公司制造，机长 9.68 米、翼展 11.38 米、机高 3.23 米，装 1040 马力艾利逊 V1710-33 型 12 缸液冷发动机，全重 3450 千克，最大速度 566 千米/小时，升限 9875 米，航程 1500 千米，武器 4 挺 12.7 毫米机枪。

P-40E Warhawk fighter: a single-seat plane made by American Curtiss Leiter Company in 1942; length: 9.68m, wing span: 11.38m, height: 3.23m; powered with Eilison V1710-39 type, 12-cylinder liquid cooled engine of 1,150 horse power; total weight: 3,760kg; max. speed: 569km/hr; ceiling: 8,840m; range: 1,360km; airborne weapon: six 12.7mm cannons, bomb 227kg.

P-40E“战鹰”战斗机：乘员 1 人，1942 年美国寇蒂斯·莱特公司制造，机长 9.68 米、翼展 11.38 米、机高 3.23 米，装 1150 马力艾利逊 V1710-39 型 12 缸液冷发动机，全重 3760 千克，最大速度 569 千米/小时，升限 8840 米，航程 1360 千米，武器 6 挺 12.7 毫米机枪、可带炸弹 227 千克。

The cockpit of P-40 fighter possessed the control stick and flying instruments, and its optical sight on the windscreen could raise the shooting accuracy and percentage of hits.
P-40 战斗机驾驶舱，有操纵杆，飞行仪表，风挡有光学瞄准镜，可以提高射击精度和命中率。

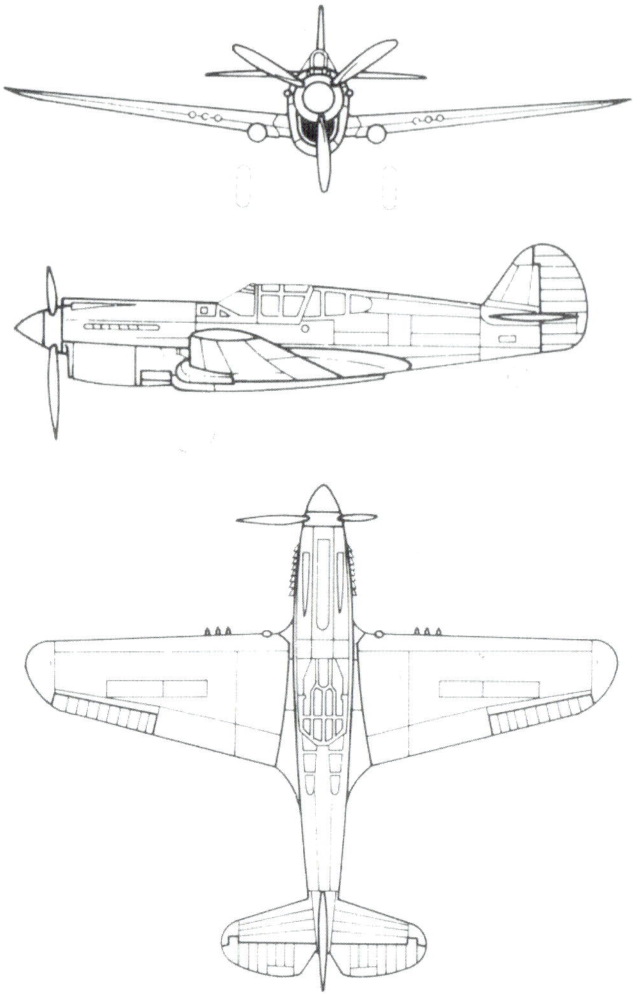

Three-view diagram of P-40C fighter.
P-40C 战斗机三面图

The P-40 fighters being painted with sign of shark eyes and teeth had become the symbol of the "Flying Tigers". The sight of such plane easily reminded people of Col. Chennault, as he won his "fame" from the group of P-40 fighters led by him.

As early as when AVG was prepared to form up, the personnel for Washington-based China Defense Supplies Inc (CDS) held discussion over what kind of symbolic sign was to be used for AVG. Some suggested a dragon, while others preferred to a hawk. Song Ziwen, who was the chief representative of CDS at that time, said that "dragon" was an ancient and obsolete concept, while "hawk" had been used by the American Air Force. So, he suggested that "tiger" be used as the sign, and testified it with an ancient Chinese idiom "add wings to a tiger". As he explained, "the tiger is the most fierce animal; and if it was added with wings, it might become even more fierce. A legend story tells that one can obtain the boldness and power of a sharp-tooth tiger if he has eaten the heart of the tiger." Therefore, AVG accepted Song's suggestion, and took a tiger with wings as the sign for the Group. As both AVG's emblem and sign contain a "flying tiger", therefore, American Volunteer Group is known as Flying Tigers.

Each squadron of AVG had a name of its own: the first squadron was named "Adam-Eve", the second squadron "Angel", and the third "Panda", with a corresponding emblem painted on the aircraft.

早在筹组美国志愿队时，在华盛顿的中国防御用品公司的人员曾就志愿队的标志进行过议论，有的提议用龙，有的提议用鹰。当时在中国防御用品公司负责的宋子文说，“龙”既古老又陈旧，“鹰”为美国空军标志容易混淆。他建议用“虎”作标志，并引出中国“为虎添翼”古语。他说：“老虎是最凶猛的野兽，当给它加上翅膀老虎就更加凶猛。传说，一个人吃了剑齿虎的心，他就能获得剑齿虎的胆量和力量。”美国志愿队接受了宋子文的建议用带翅膀的虎作为该队的标志。美国志愿航空队的队徽及标志都有一只“飞虎”，因此又把美国志愿航空队称为“飞虎队”。

美国志愿队每个中队都有自己的名称，如第 1 中队称“亚当-夏娃中队”、第 2 中队称“天使中队”、第 3 中队称“熊猫中队”，并有相应的图案作为队徽喷涂在飞机上。

The original " Flying Tigers " patch of the AVG was designed in early 1942 by Walt Disney Studios. A Bengal tiger with wings was shown soaring out of a " V " for Victory.
“飞虎队”标志的原型由美国迪斯尼公司在 1942 年设计。一只展翼的孟加拉虎从代表着胜利的“V”字中飞扑而出。

Emblem of the Flying Tigers (AVG).
“飞虎队”(美国志愿航空队)队徽

Memorial sign of Flying Tigers made by the American Flying Tigers Association after the war.
战后，由美国“飞虎协会”制作的“飞虎队”纪念标志

Emblem for Adam-Eve Squadron.
“亚当-夏娃中队”队徽

Emblem for Angel Squadron.
“天使中队”队徽

Emblem for Panda Squadron.
“熊猫中队”队徽

Organization of the American Volunteer Group

美国志愿航空队组织系统图

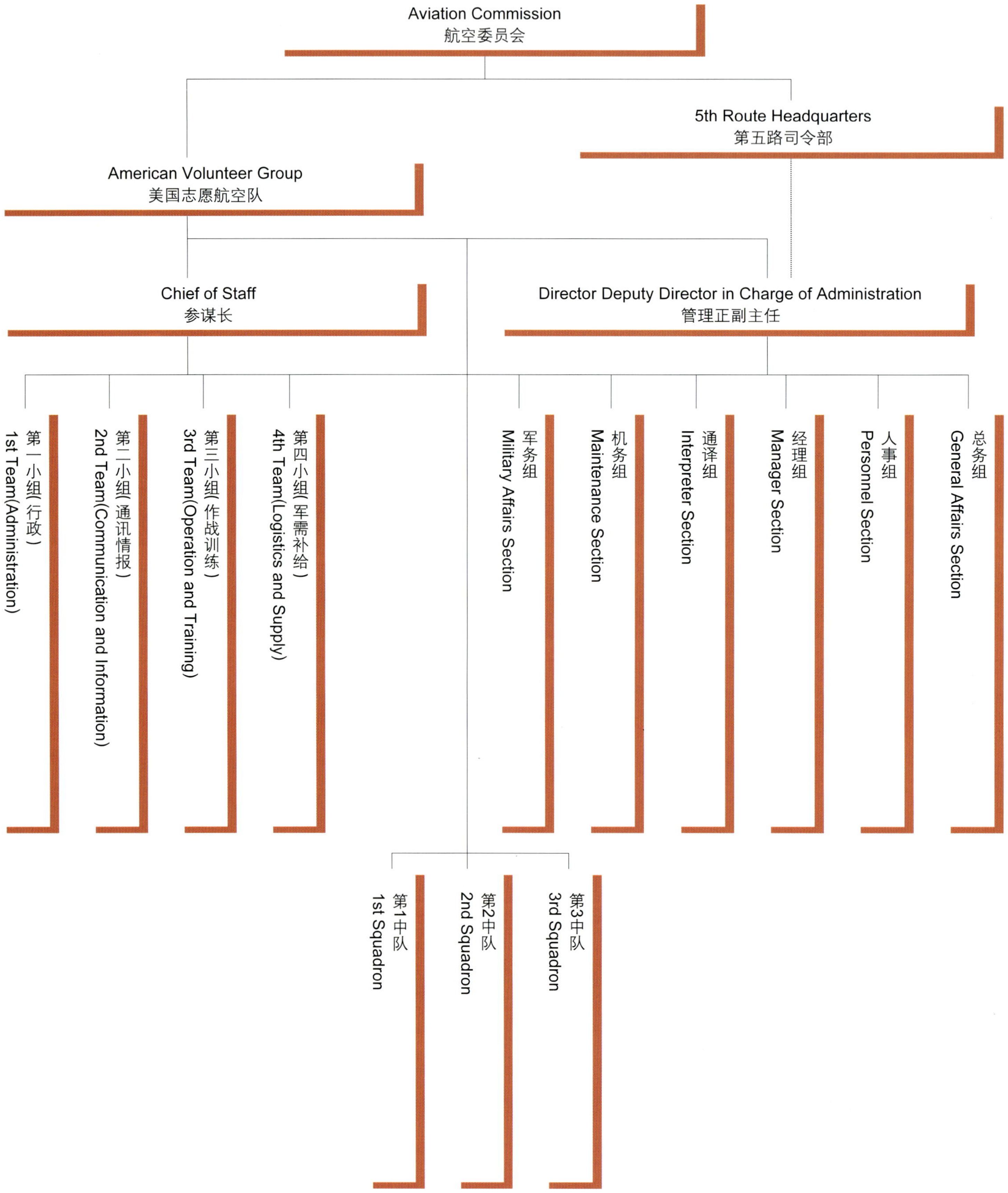

1-4

A Combat Debut of 9: 0

首战9：0获胜

JAF regarded the Burma Road – the only supply line for China – as their major target to attack. The Burma Road ended in the north at Kunming in China, ended in the south at Lashio in Burma. This gravel road extended as long as 959 km, road base width 8-9m, two-way traffic, and totally zig-zaged among the mountains. The war materials provided by the allied countries for China first arrived at Yangon through waterway, then transferred to Kunming through the Yangon-Lashio Road and the Burma Road. After October 8, 1941 when Thailand surrendered to Japan, the Japanese troops deployed fighter planes and bomber planes at the airbase in Thailand nearby the border with Burma, a substantial threat to the transportation on the Burma Road. The Japanese force attempted to destroy the Burma Road, then to take over Kunming, provincial capital of Yunnan and further Chongqing for reaching its purpose of conquering whole China. However, both the Chinese army and British troops stationed in Burma spared no effort in protecting the Burma Road; and AVG also joined in the mission of safeguarding the Burma Road. Worrying that AVG's fighters in Keydaw airbase might be stricken by the JAF, Col. Chennault transferred in emergency all of the members and aircraft to Yangon and Kunming, except for the 12 P-40 fighters that needed further adjustment and test and 25 pilots who had not finished the training on fight subjects.

日本空军空袭的主要目标是当时中国惟一的供应线——滇缅公路。滇缅公路北端是中国的昆明，南端是缅甸的腊戌，全长959千米，碎石路面，路基宽8~9米，可双向行车，完全是蜿蜒的山路。中国抗战所需的物资先由同盟国经水路运到缅甸仰光，经仰光——腊戌公路，再经滇缅公路运到中国昆明。1941年10月8日泰国投降后，日军在泰缅边境泰国一侧的空军基地部署了战斗机和轰炸机，对滇缅公路的运输构成严重的威胁。日军企图破坏滇缅公路，攻占云南省会昆明，进而攻占“陪都”重庆，达到占领全中国的目的。中国军队和驻缅甸的英国军队都全力以赴保卫滇缅公路，美国志愿队也担负了保卫滇缅公路的任务。陈纳德十分担心日军飞机空袭美国志愿队停在缅甸凯德机场的战斗机，除12架未调试完的P-40战斗机和25名没有完成战斗科目训练的飞行员外，其余的人员和飞机分别紧急转往仰光和昆明。

Supply Line for War Materials Sent from the Allied Countries through Waterway and Land Road to China.
同盟国经水路、陆路向中国运送补给物资以及滇缅公路示意图

On Dec. 18, 1941, Japanese aircraft launched a sudden bomb raid to Kunming. On Dec. 19, Col. Chennault gave order that the first and second squadrons ferry to Kunming for air defense within Yunnan Province, and the third squadron stay in Yangon to assist the British force in air-defense operation. In the morning of Dec. 20, 10 "96"/Mitsubishi G3M2 bombers of JAF took off from Hanoi, Vietnam and headed toward Kunming without necessary escort by fighters. Such a bold but imprudent action indicated that the Japanese force actually had no idea about the urgent arrival of AVG troop in Kunming. Then, AVG's 24 P-40B fighters took off for interception and an aboil air-battle took place in the sky above Kunming. Faced with a sudden strike from AVG, Japanese pilots could do nothing but meet the attack hastily. But the hulking bombers were no match for the flexible fighters; so the Japanese bombers hurried in dropping the bombs to run away. By that time, the formation of each side was in disorder, and the planes of either side were thrown into dogfight by individual. During the fight, Louis Hoffman aimed to fire against one bomber and hit the air gunner in the enemy aircraft; then he opened another fire against this bomber, and soon the bomber was seen out of control...... Frez Olf dived from higher altitude, aimed one bomber from upper rear of the enemy formation, opened fire at short distance and hit exactly the fuel tank of the enemy

1941 年 12 月 18 日，日军飞机突然轰炸昆明。12 月 19 日，陈纳德命令第 1、2 中队驻防昆明担任云南境内防空作战任务，第 3 中队留驻仰光协助英军防空作战。12 月 20 日上午，日军从越南河内起飞 10 架 96 式/三菱 G3M2 陆上轰炸机，在没有战斗机的掩护下空袭昆明。日本空军之所以这样大胆，说明日军并不知晓美国志愿航空队已于昨天紧急转往昆明。美国志愿队起飞 24 架 P-40B 战斗机拦截，在昆明上空展开了激烈空战。日军飞行员突然遭到志愿队的攻击仓促应战，笨重的轰炸机不是灵活战斗机的对手，日军轰炸机慌忙丢下炸弹逃跑。这时，双方的队形都乱了，各自为战进行单机混战。空战中路易斯·霍夫曼瞄准 1 架轰炸机，击中敌机空中射击员，他再次向敌机射击，敌机很快失去控制……弗雷兹·沃尔夫从高空俯冲下来，在敌编队后上方瞄准 1 架轰炸机近距离开火击中敌机油箱，飞机起火爆炸；他很快又瞄准 1 架轰炸机，轰炸机机尾空中射击员向他开炮，他不理会向敌机发动机射击，敌机立即爆炸，连续击落 2 架敌机。鲍勃·尼尔瞄准 1 架轰炸机，击中发动机后飞机起火，最后机尾与机身脱离掉了下去。罗伯特·桑德尔与敌机打对头，击中敌机右发动机，敌机冒着火光掉了下去。查里·邦德瞄准 1 架轰炸机，迅速扣动板机，可是什么事情也没有发生。由于兴奋他忘了

"96"/Mitsubishi G3M2 land bomber: 7 crews, manufactured by Japan Mitsubishi Industrial Company in 1937, length 16.45m, wing span 25m, height 3.68m, powered with 2×1,075 horse-power Mitsubishi "Golden Start" type-41 14-cylinder air-cooled engines, gross weight 8,000kg, max. speed 373 km/hr, ceiling 4,180m, range 4,380km, equipped with one 20mm-calibre cannon, four 7.7mm-calibre machineguns, and capable of carrying 800kg bombs.

96 式/三菱 G3M2 陆上轰炸机：乘员 7 人，1937 年日本三菱工业公司制造，机长 16.45 米、翼展 25 米、机高 3.68 米，装 2· 1075 马力三菱“金星”41 型 14 缸气冷星型发动机，全重 8000 千克，最大速度 373 千米/小时，升限 4180 米，航程 4380 千米，武器 1 门 20 毫米机炮、4 挺 7.7 毫米机枪、可带炸弹 800 千克。

AVG's Airbase in Kunming.
美国志航空愿队在昆明的基地

bomber, causing it to burn before blow-up; he soon aimed at another bomber and opened fire against the engines of the bomber, paying no attention to the firing against him from the air gunner in the tail of the bomber, and this bomber was immediately blew up. So he successively hit down two enemy planes. Bob Neil opened fire against one bomber, causing it to burn after hitting its engine; finally, the bomber's tail portion was separated away from the fuselage and fell down. Robert Sandell fought face-in-face with an enemy bomber and hit the bomber's right engine to cause it to fall down with dragging fire. Charlie Bond, however, pressed the firing button after he had aimed one bomber, but nothing happened. He then found out he was too excited to release the locking device for firing. So he made a quick breakaway, climbing and making turn to reposition himself. He re-followed the same bomber steadily and aimed for a second time to fire. The bullets hit the bomber's fuselage to cause it to blow up in the air. Eide Rectol tried to fire against one bomber at short distance after he had aimed it, but he nearly collided with the bomber; so he immediately pushed forward the control stick to go under the bomber. Then he caught up with the same bomber and opened fixed fire against the bomber. This injured bomber kept its position in the

Chinese technicians had a group-picture taken before P-40 fighter of AVG.
中国地勤人员在美国志愿航空队 P-40 战斗机前合影留念

The overwhelming victory in the first air-battle tremendously encouraged the morale of AVG members. The pilots of the second squadron happily had a group-picture taken before P-40 fighter, holding with the emblem of Angel Squadron.
首战胜利，极大的鼓舞了志愿队队员，第 2 中队的队员们拿着"天使中队"队徽在 P-40 战斗机前合影留念。

formation for quite a long period of time before it finally fell down to the ground. Eide Rectol then ran after another bomber, but later he ran into disorientation. He had no navigational chart to help him. So he set inbound course after confirming the heading of the airbase. The fuel was finally run out of and he had to make a forced landing on a wheat field. He returned to the airbase with help from the local people. The Japanese bombers were by no means to compete with the faster and more aggressive P-40 fighters, and the American Volunteer Group made its first debut in the air battle with an excellent result of 9: 0. For the JAF on the other hand, it was its first experience of disastrous defeat since its presence in China two years ago. The news of victory soon spread over every corner of China. As all of the aircraft of AVG were marked with a tiger with wings, the media in China addressed AVG as "Flying Tigers". The splendent result in the air battle proved that each member of the Flying Tigers possessed himself with the boldness and power of tiger. Before long, the news got around in America, where the local media also reported the performance of the American Volunteer Group. During the war of resistance against Japan, the name of Flying Tigers was widely known, due to its outstanding performance.

打开保险。他迅速脱离敌机，上升转弯，重新占位，又重新稳定跟踪上刚才那架敌机，瞄准射击，子弹击中敌机机身凌空爆炸。埃德·雷克托瞄准 1 架轰炸机，为了近距离开火，差点和敌机相撞。他猛地推杆钻到了敌机下面，再次撵上那架轰炸机，一个点射击中敌机，这架轰炸机在编队中飞了好长时间才坠落在地。埃德·雷克托又去追赶另 1 架敌轰炸机，飞了一阵后迷航了，他没有航图，在确定返回基地的航向后就往回飞，最后油料耗尽在一片麦地迫降，在当地群众的帮助下回到了昆明基地。日本轰炸机敌不过速度快、攻击力强的 P-40 战斗机，美国志愿队以 9:0 的战绩，首开空战纪录。这是日本空军两年多来在中国战场首次遭到严厉打击，胜利的消息很快传遍了全中国。因为美国志愿队的飞机上都画有"带翼的虎"，当时中国的报刊都称美国志愿队为"飞虎队"。空战辉煌的战果证明，"飞虎队"的队员们具有"虎"的胆量和力量。这一消息传到美国，美国报刊也报道了志愿队的战绩。抗战期间，由于"飞虎队"战果累累，其名声几乎家喻户晓。

1-5

Highly Praised Flying Tigers

备受赞誉的“飞虎队”

On the morning, Dec.21, 1941, JAF sent 27 bombers to launch a bomb raid against Britain Royal Air Force's airbase in Dawei, Burma. In the afternoon, one Japanese reconnaissance aircraft sneaked in at 7,600m altitude for scout over Yangon's Mingaladon airbase. Col. Chennault immediately informed the pilots of AVG's third squadron based in Yangon that in the following two or three days the JAF might start an air attack to Mingaladon airbase, and demanded that they be well prepared for an air battle at any time.

On Dec. 23, knowing that JAF's 54 "97"/Mitsubishi Ki-21-11b land bombers, escorted by 12 "97"/Nakajima Ki-27b fighters and 8 Mitsubishi A6M2 Zero fighters were moving in for a surprise attack on Yangon, the third squadron of AVG dispatched 15 P-40s and Britain RAF sent 18 Bristol Beaufighter Mk. IF fighters to meet the attack. After taking off, the fighters of AVG's third squadron fell into two groups, respectively led by George McMelan and Park Dubon, to perform alert patrol at 5,000m altitude. JAF's bombers taken off from Bangkok and fighters taken off from Tak in Thailand were united in the sky above Bay of Martaban before heading to Yangon. As the Japanese bombers were approaching Yangon, George McMillan, who had been waiting at higher altitude, immediately led his group to dive and open heavy fire against the enemy aircraft. While R.T.Charlie Old hit the enemy's leader aircraft, the group leader George McMillan shot down two enemy aircraft in succession. R. T. Smith displayed his

1941年12月21日上午，日本空军27架轰炸机轰炸了英国皇家空军在缅甸土瓦的前进基地。下午又有日本空军1架侦察机在7600米高空，对缅甸仰光明加拉顿机场进行侦察。陈纳德立即告诉驻仰光志愿队第3中队的飞行员们，日军近两、三天可能空袭仰光明加拉顿机场，要求他们随时做好战斗准备。

12月23日，日本空军54架97式/三菱Ki-21-11b陆上轰炸机，在12架97式/中岛Ki-27b陆上战斗机和8架三菱A6M2“零”式战斗机的掩护下突袭仰光，美国志愿队第3中队起飞15架P-40战斗机、英国皇家空军起飞18架布里斯托尔“英俊战士”Mk.IF战斗机迎敌。志愿队第3中队起飞后即分为两个小组，分别由乔治·麦克米兰和帕克·杜邦率领，在5000米空中警戒巡逻。日军从泰国曼谷起飞的轰炸机和从泰国达府起飞的战斗机，在马达班湾上空汇合后向仰光飞来。当日军轰炸机低达仰光上空时，在高空等待的乔治·麦克米兰率领队员立即俯冲下来，猛烈开炮，队员R·T·查理·奥尔德击中敌带队长机，志愿队带队长机乔治·麦克米兰连续击落2架敌机，队员R·T史密斯击落1架敌机，直到子弹打完。正当乔治·麦克米兰小组与敌机打得难解难分之际，帕克·杜邦小组赶来支援，很快就击落2架敌机。尼尔·马丁带领2架 P-40从敌编队侧翼进攻，当尼尔·马丁俯冲接敌时，后上方的3架敌战斗机一

braveness by shooting down one enemy aircraft and fought to the last bullet. As George's group and the enemy formation were locked in the air battle, the other group led by Park Dubon showed up to support, hitting down two enemy aircraft in no time. Neil Martin led two P-40s to attack from side of the enemy formation. When he was making diving to fire, three enemy fighters opened fixed fire upon him from rear above. Unfortunately, his P-40 was hit and fell rolling-over down to the ground. Neil Martin became the first air-battle martyr of AVG. Before long, both AVG and Britain RAF fighters were running short of fuel and ammunition. Therefore, these two formations prepared to return to the airbases. Taking its own advantage of more number in aircraft in the sky, the enemy ran after AVG's and Britain RAF's planes on one hand, and started a bombing raid to the city of Yangon and Mingaladon airbase on the other. The enemy's Zero fighters even strafed at low-altitude against the crowded streets. Many citizens got out of their houses to see what was happening, but were resultantly shot dead or injured. The runway and many installations in Mingaladon airbase were caused damaged in the bomb raid. In this air battle, the American Volunteer Group shot down 6 enemy aircraft, at the cost of losing three aircraft and two pilots. Among the three aircraft lost, one was directly shot down, one was hit injured and the pilot bailed out before crash; the third one was shot injured in the air and later crashed into a bomb pit, and the pilot Girbert was sacrificed. Britain RAF shot down 7 enemy aircraft, at the cost of losing 11 own aircraft and 5 pilots.

齐向他开火，他的飞机被击中，翻滚着栽到地上。尼尔·马丁成为美国志愿航空队在空战中的第一位烈士。经过一番激烈空战，美国志愿队和英国皇家空军编队的油料和弹药都所剩无几，于是两个编队都准备返回基地。日军仗着飞机多有优势，一面追赶美国志愿队和英国皇家空军编队的飞机，一面对仰光城市和明加拉顿机场进行狂轰滥炸，“零”式飞机还对拥挤的街道进行低空扫射。许多市民从家中出来看热闹，结果被打死打伤，明加拉顿机场跑道及设备被炸坏。这次空战美国志愿航空队击落 6 架敌机，被击落 1 架。被击伤 2 架，其中 1 架飞行员弃机跳伞损失 1 架，另 1 架掉进炸弹坑，飞行员吉尔伯特牺牲，损失飞机共 3 架，牺牲飞行员 2 名；英国皇家空军击落 7 架敌机，被击落 11 架，牺牲飞行员 5 名。

On Dec.23, 1941, the third squadron of AVG yielded a result of shooting down 6 JAF aircraft in the air battle above Mingaladon airbase. This was a group picture taken for the pilots of the third squadron before P-40 fighter.

1941 年 12 月 23 日，美国志愿队第 3 中队在仰光明加拉顿机场上空与日机空战，取得击落 6 架敌机的战果。这是第 3 中队的飞行员在 P-40 战斗机前合影。

Bristol Beaufighter Mk.IF fighter: 2 crews, manufactured by Great Britain Bristol Aircraft Co., Ltd in 1940, length 12.50m, wing span 17.63m, height 4.83m, powered with 2×1,400 horse-power "Hercules" type-XI 14-cylinder air-cooled engines, gross weight 9,500kg, max. speed 516 km/hr, ceiling 8,000m, range 1,890km, equipped with four 20mm-calibre cannons and six 12.7mm-calibre machine-guns.
布里斯托尔"英俊战士"Mk.IF战斗机：乘员2人，1940年英国布里斯托尔飞机股份有限公司制造，机长12.50米、翼展17.63米、机高4.83米，装2·1400马力"大力士"XI型14缸气冷星型发动机，全重9500千克，最大速度516千米/小时，升限8000米，航程1890千米，武器4门20毫米机炮、6挺12.7毫米机枪。

On Dec. 25, 1941, the Christmas Day, JAF dispatched 60 "97" bombers escorted by 18 Zero fighters to attack Yangon. P-40 fighters of AVG took off for interception and shot down 12 enemy aircraft. In order to diminish its loss, JAF changed its tactics and launched night attack instead. In response, the Britain RAF took over the task of air-defending Yangon at night, while AVG launched sudden attacks on the Japanese airbases in Thailand during day time. On Jan.10, 1942, AVG called out 9 P-40s, together with Britain RAF's 6 fighters, to attack one of JAF's airbases in Thailand, destroying 24 enemy aircraft and 3 trucks, and strafing Japanese ground troops. After Singapore was conquered in mid-February, JAF strengthened its air attacks against Yangon, and dispatched more than 100 aircraft each day for attacking Yangon in waves. On Feb. 25, Japanese ground forces started a general offensive against Yangon, and 200 JAF's aircraft were in the sky for supporting the ground forces. But AVG and Britain RAF only had 15 fighters in total to meet the attack. Through arduous struggle, AVG pilots shot down 12 enemy aircraft. On Feb. 26, JAF launched a new round of attack on Yangon with 200 aircraft, but AVG had only 6 P-40s remained. In this round of fighting, AVG shot down another 12 enemy aircraft, bringing no damage or loss to own side. On Feb. 27, AVG was forced to withdraw from Yangon and move northward to Magway airbase nearby Ayeyarwady River, about 400km away from Yangon.

1941年12月25日圣诞节，日本空军出动"九七"式轰炸机60架，在18架"零"式飞机的掩护下空袭仰光，美国志愿队起飞拦截，击落敌机12架。为了减少损失，日本空军改变了战术，改为夜间袭击。仰光的夜间防空作战任务由英国皇家空军担负，美国志愿队则在白天突击泰国境内的日军机场。1942年1月10日，美国志愿队出动P-40战斗机9架同英国皇家空军6架飞机空袭了日军在泰国的一个空军基地，击毁敌机24架、卡车3辆，并扫射了敌人部队。2月中旬新加坡陷落后，日军加强对仰光的空袭，每天出动100多架飞机轮番袭击仰光。2月25日，日军地面部队开始对仰光发起总攻，出动200架飞机协同地面部队作战，美国志愿队和英国皇家空军只有15架飞机应战，经过艰苦奋战，美国志愿队击落敌机12架。26日日军出动200架飞机再次空袭仰光，美国志愿队只有6架P-40飞机可以参战，空战中美国志愿队又击落敌机12架，自己无一伤亡。27日美国志愿队被迫撤出仰光，移驻仰光以北400千米伊洛瓦底江畔的马圭基地。

"96"/Mitsubishi G3M2 land bomber: 3 crews, manufactured by Japan Mitsubishi Industrial Company in 1941, length 7.53m, wing span 11.31m, height 3.25m, powered with 2×1,530 horse-power type-Ha-101 14-cylinder air-cooled engines, gross weight 10,632kg, max. speed 486 km/hr, ceiling 5,000m, range 2,800km, equipped with one 20mm-calibre cannon and four 7.7mm-calibre machineguns, and capable of carrying 1,000kg bombs.
96 式/三菱 Ki-21-11b 陆上轰炸机：乘员 3 人，1941 年日本三菱工业公司制造，机长 7.53 米、翼展 11.31 米、机高 3.25 米，装 2· 1530 马力 Ha-101 型 14 缸气冷星型发动机，全重 10632 千克，最大速度 486 千米/小时，升限 5000 米，航程 2800 千米，武器 1 门 20 毫米机炮、4 挺 7.7 毫米机枪、可带炸弹 1000 千克。

On March 21, 1942, JAF launched a large-scale air attack on Magway airbase, causing great loss to AVG.
1942 年 3 月 21 日，日军对美国志愿队马圭基地进行大规模空袭，造成不小的损失。

On March 21, escorted by 20 Zero fighters, JAF's 54 "97"/ Mitsubishi Ki-21-11b land bombers launched a surprise attack on Magway airbase, causing a loss of 6 P-40s to AVG. Upon hearing news in Kunming, Col. Chennault decided to give the Japanese a retaliative lesson. On Mar.23, AVG's 10 Kunming-based P-40 fighters placed an unexpected close call to the JAF's airbase in Chiangmai, Thailand, setting the whole airbase on fire, and destroying all of the 40-odd JAF bombers and fighters on ground. Then at that time, Chinese Government purchased 20 modified P-40E fighters and delivered them to AVG.. On hearing that the Army Air Force, some air and ground crew were unwilling to live a tight life of regular forces,and resigned from their posts.By the mid April, AVG totally had 21 air and ground crews, 36 active fighters, and 39 fighters under repair.

3 月 21 日，日军 54 架 97 式/三菱 Ki-21-11b 陆上轰炸机在 20 架“零”式战斗机的掩护下，突然袭击了马圭基地，美国志愿队损失 6 架 P-40 战斗机。陈纳德在昆明接到这一消息，决定对日军进行报复。3 月 23 日，驻昆明的美国志愿队 10 架 P-40 战斗机突然袭击了日军在泰国的清迈机场，整个机场一片火海，40 余架日军的轰炸机和战斗机全部摧毁在地面。这时，中国政府又从美国购买 20 架改进型 P-40E 战斗机，交给美国志愿队。因听说志愿队将归并陆军航空队，有些队员不愿再过正规部队的紧张生活而自动离职。到 4 月中旬，美国志愿队共有空、地勤人员 21 人，作战飞机 36 架，正在修理的飞机 39 架。

Dark Haidman, pilot of AVG's third squadron, soon learned how to use the air guerrilla tactics created by Chennault. He happily had a picture taken in front of P-40 fighter.
美国志愿队第 3 中队飞行员达克·海德曼很快就掌握了陈纳德的空中游击战战术，高兴之余他在 P-40 战斗机前照相留念。

Chennault-led AVG resorted to a guerrilla way of Hit and Run for their surprise attacks on JAF's airbase in Thailand and Burma. Regarding to this, JAF decided to take retaliatory measure and kept on attacking AVG's airbase. In order to minimize the possible loss, AVG kept on ferrying from one airbase to the other, so as to puzzle JAF where AVG actually was. Meanwhile, AVG created P-40 -alike targets, filled them up with dry grass and displayed them in the airbase. So when JAF' pilots found those "targets" and dropped bombs over them, they would be burning up, convincing the JAF that the targets had been destroyed.

When Magway airbase was taken over by Japanese forces, AVG transferred to Leiyun inside Yunnan nearby the border. In Leiyun, there was an aircraft repair factory moved from Hangzhou. April 29 was the birthday of Mikado, and Chennault anticipated that JAF might attack Leiyun one day before the Mikado's birthday. So he ordered AVG pilots to be prepared for air battle. As expected, in the early morning of April 28, JAF dispatched 27 "97"/Mitsubishi Ki-21-11b land bombers and a number of Zero fighters to attack Leiyun airbase. But in the sky were the P-40 fighters of AVG waiting for the enemy to come. AVG's fighters, after successfully fulfilling the mission without a single aircraft lost and instead of going back to Leiyun, landed cleverly at an auxiliary airbase nearby Mangshi. While JAF's formation, being unexpectedly attacked by the P-40 fighters on the way, lost 8 aircraft. The very same day, Japanese army force conquered Lashio, Burma's important town in the north and the start point of the Burma Road. The fall of Lashio into enemy's hand caused not only the cut-out of the important international transport line -- the Burma Road, but also placed the Yunlei-based AVG into danger. So, AVG had to burn down the 22 P-40 fighters that were being repaired in the factory before withdrawing to Baoshan and Yunnanyi airbases.

陈纳德的志愿队对日军在泰国和缅甸的空军基地进行突然袭击，采取“打了就跑”的游击战术。为此，日军采取报复措施，不断空袭美国志愿队的基地。为了减少损失，志愿队在几个基地之间不停地转移，日军搞不清美国志愿队到底在哪里。同时，在机场放上装满干草的假 P-40 飞机。当日军发现目标并进行轰炸时，它们就会燃烧起来，使人信以为真。

马圭基地被日军攻占后，美国志愿队移驻中缅边境云南境内的垒允，这里有一座从杭州迁来的飞机修理工厂。4 月 29 日是日本天皇的诞辰日，陈纳德估计日军会在前一天袭击垒允，他命令志愿队做好战斗准备。果然 4 月 28 日早晨，日军出动 27 架 97 式/三菱 Ki-21-11b 陆上轰炸机和大批“零”式战斗机攻击垒允基地。志愿队的 P-40 战斗机早已在空中待战，完成任务后不回垒允，而在芒市一个辅助机场降落。日军飞机在途中遭到 P-40 战斗机的突然攻击，被击落 8 架，而美机无一损失。当天，日本陆军攻占缅北重镇腊戍，这是滇缅公路缅甸境内的起点。腊戍的陷落，不仅使滇缅公路这一重要国际交通线被切断，也使美国志愿队在垒允的处境十分危急。他们被迫焚毁了正在垒允修理厂修理的 22 架 P-40 战斗机，撤退到云南保山、云南驿等基地。

After the taking over of Lashio, the Japanese troops moved all the way north along the Burma Road. On May 3, the Japanese troops conquered Wanding, the important frontier town of Yunnan. Soon, they moved further forward to reach at the west bank of Nujiang River. In withdrawing, the Chinese troops destroyed the iron-cabled bridge across the River. But the Japanese troops brought necessary bridge-making appliances with them and attempted to move across the river. The Nujiang River served as a natural barrier between China and Burma; and the Japanese troops would move directly forward to enter Kunming if they broke through this natural fortification. The broken bridge across the Nujiang River, as well as Chennault-led Flying Tigers, were the impediments for the Japanese troops on their way to Kunming. On May 4, JAF dispatched 50 bombers and fighters to bomb the Baoshan airbase. Charlie Bond took off individually to intercept and shoot down two enemy aircraft. Ben Foshee, however, was hit by a bomb and died in his fighter when he was preparing to take off. May 5, Japanese aircraft attacked again on the Baoshan airbase. And this time, 9 AVG's P-40 fighters took off for interception, and shot down 9 enemy aircraft. May 6, Chiang Kai-shek ordered Col. Chennault's AVG to spare no effort in attacking Japanese ground troops between Nujiang River and Longling. During May 7–9, AVG sent 4 P-40C and 4 P-40E fighters to open fierce fire against the Japanese troops in the valley of Nujiang River. Meanwhile, Chinese Air Force also joined in the battle and dispatched more than 20 sorties of fighters to bomb and strafe the Japanese troops in Longling, Mangshi, Lashio and the west bank of the Nujiang River, leaving behind disastrous casualty of the Japanese troops. The Japanese troops had to withdraw back to Longling. Since then, the Japanese troops and Chinese troops were pushed to a stalemate at the separate side of the Nujiang River for more than 2 years, and the Japanese troops made no way in crossing over the river for moving forward.

May 12, being informed that JAF's aircraft were concentrating in Jialin airbase of Hanoi Vietnam, AVG spared no time to send 10 P-40 fighters and destroy 16 enemy aircraft. As the situation in the theatre changed, the Japanese ground forces moved northward, and AVG's team in Burma also gradually transferred northward to Yunnan China.

But the Japanese troops attempted to press up to Kunming – the key place where China meant to maintain protracted war against Japan. And this was very reason why Chennault located AVG's headquarters and airbase in Kunming. So, AVG sent another 5 P-40 fighters to Baoshan airbase for safeguarding AVG's vehicle team withdrawing from Burma; and set up a radio station and one logistic branch at Yunnanyi, a town located in-between Baoshan and Kunming, for providing logistic support for P-40 fighters flying by.

日军攻占腊戍后，沿滇缅公路长驱直入，5月3日，日军占领云南边境重镇畹町。很快，日军已抵进怒江西岸，中国军队在退却时破坏了连接怒江两岸的铁索桥，但日军带有架桥器材企图架桥强渡怒江。怒江是横在中、缅两国之间的一道天然屏障，如果日军突破怒江天险，敌人将长驱直入进入昆明。怒江上的断桥和陈纳德的“飞虎队”成为日本人通往昆明道路上的障碍。5月4日，日军出动50架轰炸机和战斗机对保山基地进行轰炸，志愿队查理·邦德单机起飞拦截，击落2架敌机。本·福希在登机准备起飞时，被日机炸死。5月5日，日机再次空袭保山基地，志愿队起飞9架P-40战斗机拦截，击落敌机9架敌机。5月6日，蒋介石命令陈纳德的美国志愿队全力以赴袭击怒江与龙陵之间的敌军。5月7日至9日，美国志愿队出动P-40C和P-40E各4架，猛烈袭击怒江峡谷中的日军。同时，中国空军也连续出动20余架次战斗机，轰炸、扫射龙陵、芒市、腊戍及怒江西岸的日军，日军伤亡惨重，不得不退回龙陵。此后，日军与中国军队在怒江两岸隔江相持两年之久，日军没有能够再前进一步。

5月12日得知日本空军飞机在越南河内嘉林机场集结，美国志愿队出动10架P-40战斗机空袭，击毁敌机16架。随着战局的变化，日军地面部队向北推进，在缅甸的美国志愿队也逐渐向北面中国云南方向转移。

日军地面部队企图逼进中国进行持久战的关键地点——昆明。陈纳德将美国志愿队的指挥部和基地设在昆明，说明陈纳德非常重视昆明。美国志愿队调5架P-40战斗机进驻保山，掩护从缅甸撤出的美国志愿队车队；在保山和昆明之间的云南驿设置1个无线电台及1支后勤支队，为过往的P-40战斗机提供后勤支援。

Ground crews used a truck to support the tail of a repaired P-40 for levelling off the aircraft and calibrating the machineguns in June 1942.
1942 年 6 月，地勤人员将修复的 P-40 战斗机用卡车支撑机尾，使飞机保持水平姿态校正机枪。

Chennault's theory of double-plane and triple-plane formation (later developed to quadruple-plane formation) for air battle had not called for much attention in America, though, he daringly practised it in the air battles in China. Based upon JAF's hardcore advantage in the number of aircraft possessed and according to different characteristics in war tactics as well as in the performance of the aircraft of the both side, Chennault determined a guerrilla way of Hit and Run by using own's advantage in altitude and making a diving attack and breaking away, yielding positive results in air battles. From December 1941 to June 1942, AVG participated in the 7-month long warfare in Burma, China, Thailand and Vietnam, amounting to 56 air battles and 1,500 sorties, shooting down and destroying 297 enemy aircraft (other record showed 219 instead, among which 171 were shot down in the air; but the Japanese reported an actual loss of 89 aircraft. During war, it is normal that the report on achievement and loss provided by the opponent sides differ largely from each other), being shot down 12 aircraft in the air, and losing 61 aircraft on the ground (including the 22 aircraft burnt by AVG itself in Leiyun). Casualty for AVG: 4 killed in air fighting, 6 killed in the air by the firing from ground, 3 killed on the ground by bombing, 3 captured, and another 15 died in flight accidents. There were 32 Trump pilots (those who had shot 5 enemy aircraft and above were entitled Trump pilot),

陈纳德关于双机、三机编队（后来发展为四机编队）协同作战的思想，在美国未受到重视，但在中国战场，他却大胆地在实战中运用。他根据日本空军在飞机数量上占绝对优势及作战特点、双方飞机的性能，制定了利用高度优势俯冲攻击，采取“打了就跑”的游击战术，在空战中取得了积极战果。从 1941 年 12 月至 1942 年 6 月，美国志愿队在缅甸、中国、泰国和越南作战 7 个月，共参战 56 次，战斗出动 1500 余架次，击落、炸毁敌机 297 架（有的资料为 219 架，其中空中击落 171 架；日本人报告实际损失 89 架。战争中，敌对双方公布的战果、损失出入相当大是常有的事），被击落 12 架、地面损失 61 架（包括在垒允自行焚毁的 22 架）。人员伤亡：空战中牺牲 4 人，被地面炮火击中阵亡 6 人，地面被炸死 3 人，被日军俘虏 3 人，还有 15 人在飞行事故中殉职。产生了 32 名王牌飞行员（击落 5 架敌机的飞行员称为王牌飞行员），大多数美国志愿航空队队员获得中国政府颁发的勋章，有 15 名飞行员荣获英国和美国的优异飞行十字勋章。

陈纳德的作战指导思想及空战战术，在后来的一系列空中作战行动中证明是正确的，并逐渐为美国军方所接受。陈纳德多年来苦心探索、研究，创造的空战术，在实践中得

and most of AVG members were awarded with Honor Medal granted by Chinese Government. And 15 AVG pilots were honored with Distinguished Flying Cross from Great Britain and the U.S.A..

Chennault's guiding ideology and tactics for air war were proved correct in a series of air operations, and were gradually accepted by US armed forces. Chennault's tactics for air war, which he had been painstakingly hammering out and developing for years, was testified in the practices and at last was formally admitted by US military sector. He regarded this as the greatest honor in his life. As Chennault once said, the American Volunteer Group led by him was the most meaningful experience in his life.

AVG's first victory in the air war in Kunming aroused broadened attention from the media in the world, and later, the successive victories in the air battles in Yangon triggered the curiosity of the people worldwide. As mentioned British Prime Minister Churchill in his telegram to the British Governor in Burma, "the splendent victories by those American guys in the sky over the rice field in Burma, might compete for RAF's victories in the sky over the Kent Orchard and the beer flower field in the Battle of Britain, in term of the nature, if not in term of the scale". Many American news agencies, including United Press International, Associated Press, New York Times, Chicago's Daily News, and Times-Life magazine, sent reporters to Kunming to interview Chennault and his American Volunteer Group. Each time when a report was released, the Flying Tigers was covered with a new layer of legend. AVG members once heard a commentary being broadcasted from San Francisco-based KGEI Radio Station, in which the Flying Tigers was praised as the bravest troop in the world. In addition, this radio station aired 10 minutes for a special broadcasting of the achievements of the Flying Tigers, making the AVG members feel more proud of.

到了检验，并终于得到了军方正式认可，这是他一生中最大的荣誉。陈纳德曾经说，他领导美国志愿队，是他一生中最有意义的经历。

美国志愿队在昆明首次空战胜利受到世界报刊的广泛关注，仰光后来的空战连续取得胜利，更是激起了全世界人们的好奇心。英国首相丘吉尔向英国驻缅甸总督发电报称，"这些美国人在缅甸稻田上空所取得的辉煌胜利，如果不是在规模上，那么在性质上可与皇家空军在英伦空战的肯特果园和酒花田上空进行的空战所取得的胜利相媲美"。美国合众社、联合报社、《纽约时报》、芝加哥《每日新闻报》和《时代——生活》杂志等新闻机构都派记者到昆明采访陈纳德和美国志愿队。他们每发表一篇报道，"飞虎队"的传奇色彩就增加一层。志愿队人员曾听到旧金山KGEI电台播发的一篇评论，称"飞虎队"是世界上作战最勇敢的部队。这家电台还专门用10多分钟时间宣传"飞虎队"的战绩，使"飞虎队"队员们感到无比自豪。

AVG pilots had a group picture taken in front of P-40. Tom Heywood and Arweide were standing, while R.T. Smith, Ken Janestud, Robert Prescott, C. H. Lauclin and William Reed (from left to right) were siting on the ground.

美国志愿航空队人员在P-40战斗机前合影留念，站立者汤姆·海伍德和阿维德，坐地者(从左至右)R·T·史密斯、肯·杰恩斯代德、罗伯特·普雷斯科特、C·H·劳克林和威廉·里德。

This P-40B fighter belonging to AVG's second squadron was painted with 5 ensigns of Japan, indicating that the host of this P-40B had shot down 5 enemy aircraft. This is a picture of some members of the second squadron taken with the host of this aircraft.
这架志愿队第 2 中队 P-40B 战斗机上喷有 5 面日军军旗，说明他的主人已击落 5 架敌机。这是第 2 中队的队员们与战机的主人合影留念。

This is a P-40 fighter collected by a private collector, with painting and configuration exactly the same as an AVG's fighter of the wartime. There is a sign of Angel painted on the fuselage, showing that it was a P-40B fighter belonging to the second squadron of AVG; 7 ensigns of Japan, indicating that the pilot of this fighter shot down 7 Japanese aircraft. This P-40B fighter has been shown in various aviation exhibitions, and sometimes, it might perform demonstration flight for the audiences. It is said that there are less than 10 of such aircraft remained in the world, thus, it becomes very precious.

这是一位私人收藏家收藏的 1 架完全按照当年“飞虎队”战斗机涂装的 P-40 战斗机。从飞机涂装可以看到机身有“天使”标志，应该是美国志愿队第 2 中队的 1 架 P-40B 战斗机；驾驶舱旁有 7 面日本军旗，说明这架飞机的飞行员曾经击落 7 架日本飞机。这架 P-40B 战斗机不时出现在各种航空展览会上，有时还进行飞行表演。据说这种飞机全世界不足 10 架，十分珍贵。

These AVG members, who dedicated themselves to the war of resistance against Japan in China, have been perplexed by the fame and treatment they ought to deserve. AVG was organized and formed before the announcement of war between America and Japan through the efforts of a non-governmental institution; and the AVG members arrived in China secretly, and participated in the war as volunteers employed by Chinese Government. When the war ended, US government held that this group had nothing to do with the government, therefore, the members of this group were not eligible for veteran's treatments. Through 40-year argument, finally in July 1991, a special committee of the Department of Defense of U.S.A. ruled: the American Volunteer Group was sent to China in 1941 "for performing operational mission", and "was subject to the governing by USA armed forces from the date of USA's participation in the war; therefore, AVG's members should be regarded as active serviceman of USA. Though there were only 26 AVG members alive by the time, this World War II–resulted case could eventually reach a just conclusion. All of the Chinese people, especially those experiencing through the anti-Japanese war, felt happy for them.

这些曾为中国抗战做出过贡献的美国志愿队队员们，曾长期为自己的名誉和待遇问题而困扰。当时美日尚未宣战，美国志愿队是由非官方机构出面组建，队员们秘密抵达中国，以中国政府雇用的志愿人员名义参战。战争结束后，美国政府认为该组织与政府毫无关系，因而这些人不能享受退伍军人的待遇。他们经过长达四十多年的抗争，终于在 1991 年 7 月，经美国国防部的一个特别委员会裁定：美国志愿队 1941 年赴中国是“执行作战任务”，并“从美国参战之日起归属美国武装部队统辖”，因此志愿队队员应被视为美国军人。虽然这时志愿队军人只有 26 人还健在，但第二次世界大战留下来的一桩积案，总算有了公正的结论。中国人特别是经历过抗战时期的中国人，都为他们感到高兴。

II

第十航空队第 23 战斗机大队

The 23rd Fighter Group of 10th Air Force

2-1

The Founding of 23rd Fighter Group

组建第23战斗机大队

On Dec. 7 1941, the Japanese troops raided in a sneak the Pearl Harbor, which caused a great loss to the American forces and the declaration of war of US on Japan. The American Volunteer Group headed and commanded by Clire L. Chennault in operations in China's battlefield fought against the Japanese troops not only for China but also for the United States.

The Japanese troops expanded the invasion to the regions of South Asia and moved most the Army Air Force stationing in China as well as the Navy Air Force to the south. There were only 270 aircraft of the Army Air Force left in China. Thus, the attacking capability of the Japanese Air Force in China's battlefield was greatly weakened. In order to minimize the tensions in the Pacific region, the US after the declaration of war on Japan provided military aid to China actively, so as to make the Chinese troops to pin down the Japanese troops in the Chinese Continent.

As the war between the US and Japan had broken out, the American Volunteer Group headed by Chennault fought for the US in China's battlefield. The US government decided to incorporate the Volunteer Group into the American Army Air Force. On April 9 1942, Chennault was promoted with respect to the command of the Ministry of Defense of US from the ex-captain to interim colonel (Chennault was the colonel commander of the American Volunteer Group and his rank of colonel was appointed by the Aeronautical Commission of China.) and then further promoted to the brigadier general on April 16.

1941 年 12 月 7 日，日军突然袭击美国珍珠港，使美军遭受重大损失，美国对日本宣战。陈纳德领导和指挥的在中国作战的美国志愿航空队，不仅仅是为中国而战，也是为美国而战。

日军为向南亚地区扩张侵略，将在华陆军航空部队大量抽调南移，海军航空部队全部南移，陆军航空部队在华仅有 270 架飞机。因此，日本空军在中国战场的攻击力大大减弱。美国自对日宣战后，为减轻太平洋地区压力，积极向中国提供军事援助，使中国军队在大陆牵制日军。

美、日两国已经开战，陈纳德领导的美国志愿航空队在中国战场为美国作战。美国政府决定将陈纳德的志愿队并入美国陆军航空队。1942 年 4 月 9 日，根据美国国防部的命令，陈纳德由退役上尉晋升为临时上校（陈纳德任美国志愿航空队上校指挥官，其上校官衔是中国航空委员会任命的），4 月 16 日又晋升为准将。

当时，美国陆军第十航空队驻印度新德里，其部队分散在印度各地。1942 年 6 月，美国陆军第十航空队司令路易斯·布里尔顿少将，奉命带领部分重型轰炸机和运输机，前往中近东地区支援英军，防止德国隆美尔的机械化部队突破英军防线，占领苏伊士运河。路易斯·布里尔顿走后，由他的参谋长厄尔·内登任第十航空队司令。后因厄尔·内登回美国治病，8 月 18 日，又由中、缅、印战区指挥官约

This is the symbol of the US Army 10th Air Force. However, Chennault didn't show any interest in the symbol, because he wanted to have an independent air force commanded by himself.No symbol of the 10th Air Force could be found in places where his troops stationed.

这是美国陆军第十航空队的标志。因陈纳德还是希望有一支由他自己指挥的独立空军部队，因此对第十航空队的标志不感兴趣。在他的驻地看不到第十航空队的标志。

At that time, the American Army 10th Air Force was stationing in New Deli of India and its troops were scattering all over India. In June 1942, Maj. Gen. Lewis Brereton, commander of the American Army 10th Air Force went with an order to the Mid and Near East regions with part of the heavy bombers and transporters to support the British troops, so as to prevent the German mechanized troops headed by Rommel from breaking through the line of defense of the British troops to occupy the Suways Canal. El Neden, Chief of Staff of the 10th Air Force then succeeded Lewis Brereton as the commander. On Aug. 18, Clayton Bissel, the air-force adviser of Joseph Stilwell, commander of war zones in China, Burma and India succeeded El Neden as commander of the 10th Air Force, who went back to the United States for medical treatment.

On July 4, the American Volunteer Group disbanded formally and incorporated into the American Army 10th Air Force and became the 23rd Fighter Group affiliated to it. Four squadrons were under the 23rd Fighter Group, which were the squadrons No. 74, 75, 76 and No. 16 Fighter Squadron of the 51stFighter Group of the 10th Air Force. No. 16 Fighter Squadron of the 51st Fighter Group of the 10th Air Force stationed at the time in India. The rainy season bottled it up in the Assam Valleys and the aircraft could not go for operations for a whole summer. Chennault, by inviting one aircraft of No. 16 Fighter Squadron each time to China to "experience the operational life", moved the complete No. 16 squadron in a trick from India to the Baishiyi Airport in Chongqin in two months from June to July and kept it out of its original organizational system of army forever. No. 16 Fighter Squadron fought hands-in-hands with the squadrons of No. 74, 75 and 76 of the 23rd Fighter Group until the end of the war. Later, No. 11 Bomber Squadron equipped with B-25A took part in.

The five squadrons of the 23rd Fighter Group were deployed in airspace of 2000km stretching from Yunnanyi at the southwest of Yunnan to Kunming and further to Guilin in Guangxi and Hengyang and Linling in Hunan. Two operational airspaces, i.e. the east and west airspaces were constituted. The two squadrons stationed in Kunming and Yunnanyi bases carried out the defensive task primarily to safeguard the "Hump Route" and monitor the Japanese aircraft from the two directions of Vietnam and Burma. Two to three squadrons normally stationed at the eastern part, which carried out the offensive task mainly in the regions from Wuhan to Nanchang along the Yangzi River and further to Guangzhou and Hongkong.

瑟夫·史迪威的空军顾问克莱顿·比斯尔接任第十航空队司令。

7月4日，美国志愿航空队正式宣布解散并入美国陆军第十航空队，成为该队下辖的第23战斗机大队。第23战斗机大队下辖第74、75、76中队，包括“借用”第十航空队第51战斗机大队的第16战斗机中队，共四个中队。第十航空队第51战斗机大队的第16战斗机中队驻印度，因雨季被困在印度阿萨姆河谷，整个夏季飞机无法进行战斗。陈纳德采用每次邀请第16战斗机中队的1架飞机到中国来“体验战斗生活”的办法，在6、7两个月期间，把第16中队的全部人马从印度“骗”到重庆白市驿机场，再也没有让他们回归建制。第16战斗机中队与第23战斗机大队的第74、75、76中队并肩战斗，直到战争结束。后来又配属了装备B-25A的第11轰炸机中队。

23战斗机大队的5个中队，分布在从云南西南部的云南驿、昆明直到广西的桂林和湖南的衡阳与零陵长达2000千米的空域内，形成了东西两个作战空域。在昆明和云南驿基地的2个中队是以防御为主，保卫“驼峰航线”，监视越南和缅甸两个方向的日本飞机。东部经常驻有2~3个中队，以进攻为主，北起武汉，沿长江航线到南昌，南达广州、香港。

Pilots of the 16th Fighter Squadron moved from the 51st Fighter Group by Chennault in a trick took picture with a P-40 fighter painted with shark eyes and teeth.

这是陈纳德从第 51 战斗机大队“骗”来的第 16 战斗机中队的飞行员，与涂有鲨鱼眼睛和牙齿的 P-40 战斗机合影。

In order to carry on the "Flying Tigers" spirit of the American Volunteer Group, Chennault asked people to design a symbol reflecting the "Flying Tigers" spirit. No matter whether the 23rd Fighter Group of the American Army 10th Air Force or the American Army 14th Air Force, it used that symbol all along.
为了继承和发扬美国志航空愿队的“飞虎”精神，陈纳德请人设计了象征“飞虎”精神的标志。不论是美国陆军第十航空队第 23 战斗机大队，还是后来的美国陆军第十四航空队，都一直使用这种标志。

Brigadier General Chennault (in the middle) together with his two senior assistants in the early days of founding of 23rd Fighter Group.
第 23 战斗机大队成立之初，陈纳德准将(中)与两名高级助手在一起。

Ground personnel were loading ammunitions on P-40 fighter of the 23rd Fighter Group. 1686 rounds should be loaded once for six 12.7mm machine guns.
地勤人员在为第 23 战斗机大队的 P-40K 战斗机装子弹，6 挺 12.7 毫米机枪一次需要装 1686 发子弹。

Picture of "tiger" used to cover the logo of the Chinese Air Force on the fuselage of P-40 fighter.
当时用来临时覆盖 P-40 战斗机机身中国空军机徽的“虎”图

After the disbanding of the American Volunteer Group, the newly established 23rd Fighter group became independent from the alignment and the commanding system of the Chinese Air Force, but it still operated the aircraft of the former Volunteer Group. Pilots of the 23rd Fighter Group were taking pictures in front of P-40 fighter. The logo of the Chinese Air Force had not been changed into the logo of the American Army Air Force, but was covered with a picture of "tiger".
美国志愿航空队解散后，新成立的第 23 战斗机大队已脱离了中国空军序列和指挥系统，但仍然使用原来志愿队的飞机；第 23 战斗机大队的飞行员在 P-40 战斗机前留影，机身原中国空军的机徽来不及换成美国陆军航空队的机徽，暂时被用“虎”的图像盖住。

Besides the small amount of equipment provided by the Army 10th Air Force, the main equipment of the newly established 23rd Fighter Group were the 31 P-40C and 20 P-40E fighters of the former Volunteer Group. The aircrews and ground crews were basically what they were of the American Volunteer Group headed by Chennault. Thus, Chennault still acted as the commander of the 23rd Fighter Group, which was called openly "American Air Task Force in China".

The American Air Task Force in China, though still headed by Chennault had separated from the alignment and commanding system of the Chinese Air Force and became an allied force fighting side by side with the Chinese Air Force. By then, the Burma Road had been destroyed and controlled by the Japanese troops. The war materials needed by China in the war as well as the war materials needed by the US troops had to be transported by air through the "Hump Route". The strategic focus of the United States at the time was in Europe. The American Ministry of Defense formulated the personnel establishment and weapons equipped for the 23rd Fighter Group of the 10th Air Force and made clear the following tasks:

a. To safeguard the normal flights on the supply line of the "Hump Route";

b. To wipe out efficiently the Japanese aircraft in China;

c. To destroy the bases and facilities of the Japanese troops in China, Thailand, Indonesia, Burma and Taiwan;

d. To carry out harassing attacks at the transportation lines along the Yangzi River and Huang River as well the transportation line on the sea along the coast of China; and

e. To make a surprise attack on the supply points and aircraft manufactory factories in the rear of the Japanese troops and weaken the fighting strength of the Japanese troops.

新成立的第 23 战斗机大队，除陆军第十航空队给予少量装备补充外，其主要装备还是原志愿队 31 架 P-40C 和 20 架 P-40E 战斗机，共 51 架；基本上是陈纳德的美国志愿队原班人马，所以仍由陈纳德担任指挥官。该大队对外则称“美国驻华空军特遣队”。

美国驻华空军特遣队虽然仍由陈纳德领导，但已脱离了中国空军序列和指挥系统，成为与中国空军并肩作战的盟国部队。这时，滇缅公路已遭日军破坏并被日军所控制。中国抗战所需的物资，包括美军所需的作战物资完全由“驼峰航线”空中运输。美国当时的战略重心在欧洲，国防部根据亚洲战场，特别是中国战场的情况，制订了第十航空队第 23 战斗机大队人员编制和武器装备，并明确了主要任务。

美国陆军第十航空队第 23 战斗机大队的主要任务：

1、保卫“驼峰航线”空中补给线正常飞行；

2、有效的歼灭在中国境内的日军飞机；

3、破坏日军在中国境内及泰国、印尼、缅甸、台湾等地的基地和设施；

4、袭扰日军在长江、黄河及中国沿海的海上运输线；

5、袭击日军后方补给点及飞机制造厂，削弱日军的战斗力。

After the American Volunteer Group was re-designated into the 23rd Fighter Group of the American Army 10th Air Force, its operational dispatch of aircraft was affected due to the lack of the supplies and that almost all the engines of P-40 fighter were needed to be overhauled. By the end of Sept. 1942, there were only 38 pilots and 34 usable aircraft in the American Air Task Force in China, and the fuel left was only good enough for the consumption in two days. The gap between the American Air Task Force in China and the Japanese Air Force in terms of the number of aircraft was thus widened. The Japanese Air Force was equipped with more than 200 aircraft. Chennault had no way but the following to deal with the Japanese Air Force, i.e. to carry out the effective and active attacks in the right time and adopt the guerrilla strategy of "Hit and Run" to carry out surprise attacks and maneuver operations. Though the Japanese Air Force was in the position of priority in terms of aircraft number, it was inferior in position as compared with Chennault in air-combat strategies. Therefore, the American Air Task Force in China could still win success constantly in the operations with the Japanese Air Force.

Things changed better when it was in Oct. In Oct. 1942, the American Army Air Force replenished the fighter group with 20 experienced fighter pilots who had a year experience of flying in Panama and 60 aircrews of bomber aircraft as well as 20 P-40K fighters and 12 B-25A bombers.

美国志愿队改编为美国陆军第十航空队第23战斗机大队后，由于供应短缺及所有P-40飞机的发动机寿命已到需要大修等原因，影响了战斗出动，到1942年9月底，美国驻华空军特遣队仅剩下38名飞行员，34架能使用的飞机，汽油也只够使用两天。美国驻华空军特遣队与日本空军在数量上的差距正在拉开。其对手日本空军拥有200多架飞机。陈纳德对付日本空军的办法是适时有效的主动发起攻击，采用游击战术——“打了就跑”，进行奇袭和机动作战。尽管日本空军在飞机数量上占优势，但陈纳德却在空战战术上占优势。因而美国驻华空军特遣队在与日本空军作战中，仍然能够不断取得胜利。

到了10月份，情况有所好转。1942年10月，美国陆军航空队给该队补充了20名曾在巴拿马飞行过一年，有经验的战斗机飞行员和60名轰炸机机组人员，以及20架P-40K战斗机和12架B-25A轰炸机。

Brigadier General Kerlaiton Biser, commander of the 10th Air Force (right) inspected the 23rd Fighter Group. He met Brigadier General Chennault (at center) and Colonel Robert Sket of the 23rd Fighter Group in Kunming Base.
第十航空队司令克莱顿·比斯尔(右)准将到第23战斗机大队视察，在昆明基地会见陈纳德(中)准将及第23战斗机大队的罗伯特·斯科特上校。

2-2

Ready to experience "Life of Fight"

体验"战斗生活"

The constant reports by newspapers, magazines and radio programs about Chennault and his "Flying Tigers" group made both the American military personnel and civilians have profound understandings about Chennault and his "Flying Tigers" group. The "Flying Tigers" group headed by Chennault, of which the personnel was not great in number and the equipment possessed was not good at all, fought against the Japanese Air Force, whose equipment possessed was great in number and aircraft performance was better in the battlefields in China and achieved a remarkable success, which inspired greatly the American military personnel and civilians. Both the American military personnel and civilians envied them. The non-regular guerrilla type of operational strategy created by Chennauly specially attracted many pilots, who wanted to have a chance to experience the "operational life" personally in the"Flying Tigers" group.

Colonel Robert Sket, a graduate from the West Point Military Academy learnt how to fly after being enrolled into the American Army Air Force. He had flown several types of aircraft and had an experience of long-time flying fighter aircraft. Later, he was transferred to the Army Transport Command and flew C-47 transporter along the "Hump Route" to transport war materials to China for months. He once flew together in operations with the pilots of the "Flying Tigers" group and had been longing for quite a time to join the "Flying Tigers" group. His dream finally came true when he was transferred to the American Air Task Force in China. Robert Sket soon became the capable assistant of Chennault and scored great successes in the American Air Task Force in China.

报纸、杂志、电台等媒体连续不断地报道陈纳德与"飞虎队"的事迹，使美国军人和民众对陈纳德与"飞虎队"有了比较深刻的认识。陈纳德领导的"飞虎队"，人员不多、装备也不算好，在中国战场上与装备数量多、飞机性能比较好的日本空军作战，取得了丰硕的战果，极大的鼓舞了美国军民。在人们的心目中，陈纳德是英雄，"飞虎队"是英雄的战斗集体。美国民众都非常敬佩他们，美国军人都十分羡慕他们。特别是陈纳德的非正规游击式空战战术，更是吸引了许多飞行员，都想到"飞虎队"亲身体验一番"战斗生活"。

罗伯特·斯科特上校，美国西点军校毕业，加入美国陆军航空队学习飞行，飞过好几种机型，具有长时间驾驶战斗机飞行的经历。后来他调入陆军航空运输队，驾驶 C-47 运输机飞越驼峰航线，向中国运送作战物资已有几个月了。他曾经与"飞虎队"的队员们一起进行过战斗飞行，很早以前他就想加入"飞虎队"这个战斗集体。后来，他调入美国驻华空军特遣队，终于如愿以偿。在美国驻华空军特遣队，罗伯特·斯科特很快成为陈纳德的得力助手并取得丰硕的战果。

由于"飞虎队"名声在外，许多美国飞行员都向往成为一名"飞虎队"队员。所以新补充来的飞行员积极性很高，很快就适应了新的环境和新的生活。他们对陈纳德提倡的"打了就跑"的游击战术和"俯冲攻击"方法非常感兴趣，都想亲自试一试。在飞行训练和实战中，这些飞行员很快就掌握了这些战术和方法，在战斗中都取得了很好的战果。

Group photo of all aircrews and ground crews of 74th Squadron of 23rd Fighter Group.
第 23 战斗机大队第 74 中队的全体空、地勤人员合影

Because the "Flying Tigers" group had a good reputation, many American pilots had a wish to become a member of it. Thus, the newly coming pilots had high initiatives and could adapt themselves soon to the new environments and new life there. They showed interests in the guerrilla strategy of "Hit and Run" and the way of diving attack put forward by Chennault and wanted to have a try personally. They mastered the strategy and the attack way soon in flight trainings and operations and scored good successes in operations.

In confronting with the Japanese Air Force that was in superiority, Chennault thought all the time how to deal with the enemy's short points with his strong points and tried to improve constantly the strategic means to defeat the Japanese troops more effectively. The high-altitude performance of the Zero fighter of Japan after modification was very good, but the most favorite flight altitude of P-40 fighter was 4500—5500m and its operational efficiency was greatly reduced when it flew above 6000m. Chennault then thought out of a tactic, i.e. to employ B-25A bombers of the 11th Squadron as baits to carry out bombing at the altitude of 4500m and concentrate P-40 fighters at the altitude of 5500m to be alert for operation. The Japanese Zero fighters if attacking on the American bombers would sacrifice its superiority in altitude to fly to the optimum operational altitude of P-40 fighters.

In order to lure the Japanese aircraft into the "trap", the American Air Task Force in China should attack on an important

面对处于优势的日本空军，陈纳德总是在思考如何以己之长击敌之短，不断改进战术手段，更有效地打击日军。日本经过改进的“零”式战斗机高空性能比较好，而P-40战斗机最适宜的飞行高度在4500~5500米，超过6000米，其作战效能就会大大减低。陈纳德设计了这样一种战术，用第11中队的B-25A轰炸机作为诱饵，在4500米高度进行轰炸，而将P-40战斗机集结在5500米高度待战。这样，日本“零”式战斗机为了要攻击美国轰炸机，势必会牺牲高度上的优势，低飞到P-40战斗机最佳战斗高度上来。

为了使日本飞机落进入“陷阱”，美国驻华空军特遣队需要进攻一个迫使日军不能不防守的重要目标，这个目标最后选定为香港。1942年10月24日，由第11中队中队长塔克斯·希尔率领12架B-25A轰炸机，在10架P-40K战斗机掩护下，从桂林起飞轰炸香港。日本广播电台曾对香港市民说，美国轰炸机没有什么可怕，因为飞机是由一个衰老不堪的运输机飞行员海恩斯驾驶的。加勒伯·海恩斯被日本人的嘲弄激怒了，他自己掏钱印制了用中文和日文书写的“这些炸弹就是那个衰老不堪的运输驾驶员海恩斯赠送的”传单，同炸弹一起投到香港。当塔克斯·希尔率领的12架B-25A轰炸机投完炸弹准备返航时，日军从广州方面起飞26架“零”式战斗机追赶美国轰炸机。在高空担任护航的10架P-40K战斗机，背着太阳冲向“零”式战

The ground crews of the 23rd Fighter Group at Kunming Base were repairing aircraft parts on simple and crude wooden support. The logo on P-40 fighter at back had been changed into the logo used in 1942 by the American Army Air Force.
第 23 战斗机大队在昆明基地的地勤人员在简陋的木架上维修飞机部件，后面 P-40 战斗机的机徽已换成美国陆军航空队 1942 年使用的机徽。

target that the Japanese troops had to defend. And that target was finally selected as Hongkong. On Oct. 24,1942, twelve B-25A bombers headed by Tarkis Xier squadron leader of the 11th Squadron took off from Guilin to bomb Hongkong under the escort of ten P-40K fighters. The Japanese broadcast station once told the Hongkong people that the American bomber was not worthy of being afraid of, because it was flown by Haines, an old and feeble pilot. Calerb Haines, who was infuriated by the Japanese ridicules, printed with his own money the leaflet in Chinese and Japanese saying that "these bombs are presented by Haines an old and feeble pilot of transporter" and dropped them together with bombs onto Hongkong. When the twelve B-25A bombers headed by Tarkis Xier were about to perform the homeward flight after dropping off all bombs, 26 Japanese Zero fighters took off from Guangzhou to chase after the American bombers. The ten P-40K fighters carrying out the escort task flew into the group of the Zero fighter behind the sun and disrupted the formation of the Japanese aircraft. After a fierce air combat, the American Air Task Force in China lost one B-25A bomber, but both the Chinese intelligence department and the Japanese broadcast station proved that the Japanese lost twelve Zero fighters. That operational activity of bombing Hongkong was the best reflection of the air-

斗机机群，打乱了日机编队。经过一场激烈地空战，美国驻华空军特遣队损失 1 架 B-25A 轰炸机，而中国情报部门及日本电台都证实日军损失 12 架“零”式战斗机。这次轰炸香港作战行动，是陈纳德轰炸机和战斗机混合编队空战战术的最好体现。

日军飞机夜间偷袭给美国驻华空军特遣队造成过一些损失。为了打击夜间偷袭的日本轰炸机，美国驻华空军特遣队在没有夜间作战的飞机，机场没有夜航设备的情况下，大胆地使用 P-40 昼间战斗机在跑道两边摆上桐油灯为飞机起飞、降落指示方向，从而开始夜间作战。美国飞行员在地面无线电引导指挥下，搜索、跟踪目标，利用敌机发动机排气管喷出的火光进行瞄准、攻击，击落敌机。美国驻华空军特遣队开创了使用 P-40 战斗机，在夜间击落敌机的纪录。这在美国其他航空队部队是绝对不允许的，因为违反战斗条令。陈纳德敢于打破条条框框，因势利导，不断探索，创新空战战术的精神，深受飞行员们的好评。这也是陈纳德能够吸引许多飞行员加入到他的战斗集体的原因之一。

在对日本空军的作战中，当时美军虽然缺少地面雷达，但是美国驻华空军特遣队的飞机很少被敌人摧毁在地面。

combat tactics of mixed formation of bombers and fighters put forward by Chennault.

The raid in sneak by the Japanese aircraft caused certain losses to the American Air Task Force in China. In order to take strong measures against the Japanese bombers carrying out sneak raid at night, the American Air Task Force in China boldly employed the daytime P-40 fighters in case there were no aircraft for nighttime operations available and there were no night flight facilities at the airports. They put tung-oil lamps along the two sides of the runway to indicate directions for takeoff and landing aircraft. The American pilots searched and tracked targets under the guidance of ground radio stations and aimed at and attacked the enemy's aircraft with the help of the flame from the exhaust pipes of enemy's aircraft. The American Air Task Force in China opened the record of shooting down the enemy's aircraft with P-40 fighter at nighttime. This way of doing however was strictly forbidden in other air force troops in the United States, because it went against the operational regulations. Chennault was highly praised by pilots because he had the courage to break with the conventions, make the best use of the situation to explore constantly and renovate air-combat tactics. That was also the reason why Chennault could attract many pilots to join in his group.

In the operations with the Japanese Air Force, the enemy could seldom destroy the aircraft of the American Air Task Force in China on the ground even though the American troops were lack of ground radars at the time. This was mainly because Chennault had set up the air alarming net with the help of the intelligence networks of the Chinese troops and the civilians in China. That network covered the whole country. Chinese who had received special training were hired as the air surveillance personnel who reported the information about the types, number, flight altitudes and directions of the Japanese aircraft step by step or orally or through telephone to the local Chinese troops or the Chinese troops stationing nearby. Then, the Chinese troops concerned reported the information to the Americans through telephone or telegraph. Some Chinese out of hatred for the Japanese Fascists reported to the Americans initially about the situation and tendency of the Japanese Air Force. In this way, it was possible for Chennault to know about the raids of the Japanese aircraft several dozens of minutes or even several hours ahead of time. The aircraft of the American Air Task Force in China could fly to the alternate airports to hide themselves almost every time before the raid of the Japanese aircraft, or became airborne to strike against the Japanese aircraft with respect to the air situations. The loss of aircraft on ground could thus be reduced effectively. It met the Chinese situation, could be carried out easily and was very effective to set up the air-intelligence network of man in China. This could be said that it was the pioneer work done by Chennault.

The Chinese soldier hidden in thatched shed was reporting through telephone to the American troop about the types, number, flight altitudes and directions of the Japanese aircraft.
在茅草屋内隐蔽的中国军人用电话向美军报告，日军飞机出动的机型、架数，飞行高度、方向等情报。

其主要原因是陈纳德利用中国军队的情报网和中国民众，在中国建立了空中警报网。这个网络遍布全中国，雇佣经过培训的中国人充当对空监视员，他们将观察到的日军飞机的机型、架数，飞行高度、飞行方向等情报，逐级或直接用口头或电话告诉当地或附近中国驻军，中国部队再用电话或电报报告美国人。有些中国人出于对日本法西斯的憎恨，主动将所知道的日本空军情况及动向告诉美国人。这样，陈纳德可以提前几十分钟，甚至几小时，就知道有日本飞机来袭。美国驻华空军特遣队的飞机几乎在每次日本飞机空袭之前，都能从基地飞到备用机场隐蔽起来，或飞到空中视情况是否与日本飞机空战，从而有效的减少了飞机在地面的损失。在中国建立人工空中警报网络，符合中国国情，简单易行，十分有效。可以说是陈纳德的一个创举。

Three PT-17 trainers were equipped in the 23rd Fighter Group. They were used mainly for trial flights for flying techniques and tactics as well for the air reconnaissance and communication. PT-17 "Kaydet" Trainer: Cabin crews of 2 people were needed. It was firstly manufactured by the US Boeing Aircraft Company in 1940. The aircraft was 9.68m in length, 11.38m of wingspan, 3.23m in height and was equipped with air-cooled radial engine of 7 cylinders of 220 "Continent" R-670-5. The overall weight of the aircraft was 1232kg, with the maximum speed of 199km/hr, the ceiling of 3415m and the range of 812km.

第 23 战斗机大队装备 3 架 PT-17 教练机，主要用于飞行技术、战术研究试飞，空中侦察和通信联络。PT-17"凯代"战斗机：乘员 2 人，1940 年美国波音飞机公司制造，机长 9.68 米、翼展 11.38 米、机高 3.23 米，装 220"大陆"R-670-5 型 7 缸气冷星型发动机，全重 1232 千克，最大速度 199 千米/小时，升限 3415 米，航程 812 千米。

B-25A "Mitchell" Medium-sized, Medium-range Bomber: Cabin crews of 5 people were needed. It was firstly manufactured by the US North American Airlines in 1941. The aircraft was 16.48m in length, 20.60m of wingspan, 4.80m in height and was equipped with air-cooled radial engines of 14 cylinders of 2x170 horsepower R · 2600-9 type. The overall weight of the aircraft was 12292kg, with the maximum speed of 507km/hr, the ceiling of 8230m and the air range of 2170km. It could carry 1360kg ammunitions and five 12.7mm machine guns.

B-25A"米切尔"中型中程轰炸机：乘员 5 人，1941 年美国北美航空公司制造，机长 16.48 米、翼展 20.60 米、机高 4.80 米，装 2· 1700 马力莱特 R · 2600-9"塞克隆"型 14 缸气冷星型发动机，全重 12292 千克，最大速度 507 千米/小时，升限 823 0 米，航程 2170 千米，武器 5 挺 12.7 毫米机枪、可带炸弹 1360 千克。

Group photo of aircrews and ground crews of the 11th Bomber Squadron of the 23rd Fighter group taken in front of B-25H bomber in summer of 1942.
第 23 战斗机大队配属的第 11 轰炸机中队的空、地勤人员，1942 年夏天在 B-25H 轰炸机前合影。

The operation finished. Members of the 23rd Fighter Group were drinking coffee and beer in club. Some members even brought their petty dogs to the party.
战斗结束后，第 23 战斗机大队队员们在俱乐部喝咖啡、饮啤酒，有的还带着自己心爱的小狗参加聚会。

The B-25G bomber modified from type C in Jan. 1943, of which the nose had been changed into non-transparent sealed fairing. One 75mm M4 light cannon gun was added with 21 rounds of cartridges carried. B-25H bomber employed T-13E-1 75mm cannon gun of which the weight had been reduced. This was the 75mm M4 light cannon at the nose of B-25G bomber.
1943 年 1 月用 C 型改进的 B-25G 轰炸机，机头改为不透明密封罩，加装 1 门 75 毫米M4 轻型加农炮，带炮弹 21 发。B-25H 轰炸机改用减重型 T-13E-1 式 75 毫米加农炮。这是 B-25G 轰炸机机头前的 75 毫米 M4 轻型加农炮。

B-25H bomber of the 11th Bomber Squadron was refueling at Guilin Base before going to bombing the position of Japanese troops.
在桂林基地的第 11 轰炸机中队的 B-25H 轰炸机正在加油，准备轰炸日军阵地。

One of the self-amusement items of the members of the 23rd Fighter Group in between the intervals of operations was to pull jinrikisha.
在战斗的间隙里,第 23 战斗机大队队员自娱自乐的一个项目就是拉黄包车。

To shoot pheasant was the hobby of some members of the 23rd Fighter Group. It could also provide something special to the food.
打山鸡,是一些第 23 战斗机大队队员的爱好,同时可以改善生活。

At this time of war, there was a sort of deep love between the Flying Tigers and the local people of Yunnan. So, they got along with each other very well.
在那战争的岁月里，“飞虎队”队员与云南百姓和睦相处，情深义重。

2-3

Excellent Pilots

飞行员个个都是好样的

A strong and united unit with combat effectiveness should be constructed by everyone concerned in addition to the leadership of the leading people. No matter whether it was the American Air Task Force in China headed by Chennault or the 23rd Fighter Group, it was a unit full of affinity and cohesion because of the personal enchantment and leading techniques of Chennault. That unit trained and fostered in a very hard and dangerous condition a batch of excellent personnel.

The 23rd Fighter Group headed by Chennault inherited the glorious tradition and the flexible tactics of the "Flying Tigers" Group. Several best pilots of the kind emerged, among whom was John Ailson, who came from Florida of America. He was dispatched to Britain in spring of 1940 to train the British pilots to fly P-40 fighters. Later, he was dispatched to the Soviet Union to train the pilots there to fly P-40 fighters. He was transferred to the Army 10th Air Force in India as a fighter pilot after he went back home. Finally, he was transferred to Kunming as a fighter pilot of the 23rd Fighter group.

Major John Ailson was dispatched to the 75th Fighter Squadron stationing in Hengyang as the assistant of Xier Baumole, the squadron leader. In the second evening soon after he came, the information from the intelligence network said that the Japanese aircraft were flying towards Hengyang. Everyone looked into the situation helplessly when the Japanese heavy bombers were above Hengyang, because no training of intercepting bombers at night had been carried out and P-40 was not a fighter suitable for night operation at all.

一个坚强、团结、有战斗力的集体，除领导者外，还要靠全体人员的共同努力。无论是陈纳德领导美国志愿航空队还是第 23 战斗机大队，由于陈纳德的人格魅力和领导才能，使这个战斗集体充满亲和力和凝聚力。这个战斗集体在非常艰苦、十分危险的环境中，培养、造就了一批优秀的人才。

陈纳德领导的第 23 战斗机大队继承了“飞虎队”的光荣传统和灵活多变的战法，涌现出一些尖子飞行员。约翰·艾力逊少校就是他们中的代表，他是美国佛罗里达州卡诺普人。1941 年春，被派往英国，负责训练英国飞行员驾驶 P-40 战斗机。随后，又到苏联，帮助训练苏联飞行员驾驶 P-40 战斗机。回国后，调到驻印度的陆军第十航空队任战斗机飞行员。他后来调到昆明，在第 23 战斗机大队任战斗机飞行员。

约翰·艾力逊少校被派到驻衡阳第 75 战斗机中队，作为希尔·鲍漠勒中队长的副手。他刚到的第二天晚上，警报网就报告，有日本飞机向衡阳方向飞来。当日本重型轰炸机飞临衡阳上空时，大家眼睁睁地看作干着急。因为当时没有进行过夜间拦截轰炸机的训练，P-40 也不是夜间战斗机。他们通常的做法是，疏散、隐蔽、伪装飞机，人员进入防空洞。在机场附近的机场上放置假 P-40 飞机，再涂些泥灰，以假乱真。让日军飞机攻击、轰炸放在机场上的假 P-40 飞机。这种办法非常奏效，日本人经常上当。

They could do nothing but to disperse, hide and camouflage aircraft and ask people to go into air-defense caves, or put some dummy P-40 aircraft near the airport to mix the spurious with the genuine. The Japanese aircraft could then be fooled to attack at or bomb the dummy P-40 aircraft put at nearby the airport. This method was very effective and the Japanese could be fooled constantly.

After the careful observation on the Japanese bombers flying over his head at night, John Ailson found that it was possible to locate, search for, track, attack at and shoot the enemy aircraft down with the help of the flame coming out of the tail pipe of the bomber. He told what he had found to Xier Baumole the squadron leader, who was also an excellent fighter pilot and once took part in the Civil War in Spain. Xier Baumole also thought that it was practicable to intercept the Japanese bombers with P-40 fighters at night.

After the careful preparations at ground and the several times of trial flights for interception at night, they became well prepared for the interception at night and began to carry out the task of night alert.

One night, the sound made by knocking the empty can came from the airport and everyone knew that the Japanese aircraft were flying towards Hengyang. Baumole and Ailson rushed to P-40 fighters in dark, checked the aircraft, started the engines with the help of weak torch lights and flew into the sky after takeoff. They constantly climbed to 2750m, 3050m and then leveled off at 3650m. They could not see each other in the air. They were searching for carefully in the air at night and could only hear the sound of the ground commander through the radio with noises that "three two-engine bombers were flying southwards from the north". Later, they heard from the radio that " it seems they are turning to fly back". The Japanese intensified the interference to the radio and they could hear nothing at all. Suddenly, Baumole and Ailson found the enemy's bombers and they flew towards to them. Ailson was in the position nearest to the enemy's aircraft and he could judge from the flames coming out of the tail pipes of the bombers that it was three bombers flying in V formation. When he sighted the bomber flying at the left, he found flame flashing at his right. That was the flame produced by the cartridge fired out by No. 3 enemy aircraft at the rear right of the leader aircraft of the enemy. The cartridges wounded the P-40E fighter flown by Ailson by going through the fuselage and hitting the compartment and engine. As soon as Ailson depressed the button of machine guns after sighting the enemy's aircraft, six 12.7mm machine guns fired simultaneously at the enemy's aircraft. The enemy's aircraft was wounded and separated from the formation. Baumole flew to the position in time and shot down the wounded enemy's aircraft. Ailson controlled his wounded aircraft and flew in a winding way to the right of enemy's leader aircraft and fired at it after sighting the enemy's aircraft that hit his aircraft. The enemy's aircraft was hit in the

约翰·艾力逊在夜空中仔细观察从他头顶飞过的日本轰炸机，他发现轰炸机排气管喷出的火光，可以确定敌机的位置，靠近、搜索、跟踪、攻击并打掉它。他把自己的想法告诉了希尔·鲍漠勒中队长，鲍漠勒也是一位出色的战斗机飞行员，曾参加过西班牙内战，他认为用P-40战斗机夜间截击日军轰炸机是可行的。

他们经过认真的地面准备，并在夜间进行过多次截击试飞，有了进行夜间作战的把握，就开始担负夜间战斗值班任务。

一天晚上，机场响起了敲打空罐头盒的声音，大家知道有日本飞机向衡阳飞来了。鲍漠勒和艾力逊摸黑跑向P-40战斗机，他们利用手电筒微弱的灯光，检查飞机、开车、滑跑、起飞，冲向夜空……他们不断爬高2750米、3050米、3650米改为平飞，在空中谁也看不见谁。他们在夜空中仔细搜索，无线电伴着杂音勉强可以听到地面指挥官的声音，“3架双引擎轰炸机正由北向南飞来”。过一会儿，又听到“看起来他们好像正在转弯，准备回去”。日本人加强了无线电干扰，什么也听不清了。突然，鲍漠勒和艾力逊发现了敌人轰炸机，他们立刻靠向敌机。艾力逊离敌机最近，从轰炸机排气管喷出的火光，可以判断是3架按倒V形编队的轰炸机。当他把瞄准具对准在左边飞行的轰炸机时，他看到他的右边有火光在闪动，那是在敌带队长机右后方敌3号机射出的枪弹的火光。艾力逊的P-40E座机被击伤了，日机的枪弹将他的飞机从机身一直扫到座舱和发动机。艾力逊瞄准敌机按动机枪按钮，6挺12.7毫米机枪一起射向敌机，敌机受伤脱离编队。鲍漠勒赶到将这架受伤的敌机击落。艾力逊驾驶受伤的座机摇摇晃晃地绕到敌带队长机的右边，向刚才击中他的那架敌机瞄准射击，击中油箱，敌机在巨大的爆炸气浪中坠落了。

前面敌带队长机正在投弹，艾力逊利用P-40战斗机速度快的特点，很快追上敌带队长机。艾力逊的飞机发动

fuel tank and dropped in a great blast of explosion.

The enemy's leader aircraft in the front was dropping bombs. Ailson quickly chased after it with the advantage of the quick velocity of P-40 fighter. The engine of the aircraft flown by Ailson was on fire with smoke. He controlled it with great efforts to track, sight and fire at the enemy's leader aircraft. The enemy aircraft was hit, lost control and fell downwards with fire. The fire on the engine of the aircraft flown by Ailson became bigger and bigger and the engine could hardly function normally. He began to descend and the engine stopped functioning at the altitude of 900m. The airport was nearby and Ailson controlled the wounded aircraft in the dark and silent air to glide towards the airport. The aircraft drifted towards the airport and he tried to restart the engine in the air. It was however out of his expectance that the engine was successfully started. Ailson was excited, but the engine flamed out in a very short period of time and could not be started again. The aircraft lost its altitude quickly and it was impossible for him to land on the runway of the airport. He did not want to drift across Xiangjiang and dropped into the crowded city center of Hengyang. He controlled with great efforts the aircraft to keep clear of a bridge and fell into the dark and cold river. He crawled out of the cockpit and swam towards the riverside. His forehead was broken by the pieces of the instrument radiator in the strike in the falling of the aircraft and blood covered his whole face. Ailson could see hazily in the moonlight the contour of the raft in the Xiangjiang. He began to swim towards the raft desperately, because it was shorter in distance as compared with the riverside. His coat was too heavy, making him sink every now and then. He swam forwards with great efforts. When he swam near the raft, a Chinese boy helped him to climb onto the raft, which carried him to the shore. Three Chinese soldiers on the shore targeted him with bayonets. They watched with their eyes in the dark night the air combat, but did not know if the survivor was a Chinese, an American or a Japanese. Ailson took out a small Chinese flag and waved it. He uttered the several Chinese words he knew and said that he was an A-M-E-R-I-C-A-N. After they were certain that he was not a Japanese, the Chinese soldiers sent him to a house for rest. He finally went back to the airport opposite to Xiangjiang the day after.

Baumole was very angry after he went back to the airport, because he thought that Ailson must have died. He headed other pilots and flew into the sky with great anger when another batch of enemy's aircraft came in a raid at the same night. The 40 Zero fighters coming in the raid obviously took revenge for the three bombers that had been shot down by the Americans. Baumole headed the ten P-40E fighters into the formation of the Zero fighters and disrupted the formation. Baumole controlled his P-40E fighter and flew directly towards a Zero fighter. The Zero fighter was not to be outdone and flew directly towards the P-40E fighter. The two aircraft flew directly

机已着火冒着浓烟，他勉强操纵飞机跟踪、瞄准，向敌带队长机开火。敌机被击中失去控制并燃烧着向下栽。艾力逊的飞机发动机火势越来越大已不能正常工作了，他开始下降高度，900 米时发动机停车。机场就在附近，在这漆黑寂静的夜空中，艾力逊驾驶受伤的座机准备空滑返回机场迫降。飞机向机场飘去，他在空中试着开车，出乎预料，居然开车成功。艾力逊一阵激动，但好景不长马上又熄火了，再也发动不起来。飞机高度掉得很快，他是不可能在机场跑道上降落了。他不想越过湘江，撞入人口密集的衡阳市区。他费力地操纵飞机避开了一座桥梁，坠入漆黑、冰冷的河水中。他爬出机舱，向岸边游去。在飞机坠落的碰撞中，他的前额被仪器散热片撕裂，满脸流着血。在月光下，艾力逊朦胧地看到连接湘江两岸城镇的木排的轮廓，他拼命向木排游去，这比游向岸边距离要近些。他身上的衣服太重了，迫使他不时下沉，他十分费力地向前游。快靠近木排时，一个中国男孩子跑过来帮助艾力逊上了木排划到岸上。岸上 3 个中国士兵端着枪用刺刀对着他，他们在黑夜中目睹了这场空战，但不知幸存者是中国人、美国人还是日本人。艾力逊从身上拿出一面小小的中国旗挥舞着，讲了一些他所知道的中国话，说他是一个“美——国——人”。中国士兵确认他不是日本人后，将他送到一所房子休息。第二天早上，他回到湘江对岸的机场。

鲍漠勒回到机场，以为艾力逊死了，他非常愤怒。当晚另一批日本飞机来袭时，他带领队员们怒吼着冲向天空。这批 40 架“零”式战斗机显然是为被美国人击落的 3 架轰炸机报仇的。鲍漠勒带领 10 架 P-40E 战斗机冲入“零”式战斗机编队，打乱了敌人的队形。鲍漠勒驾驶 P-40E 战斗机向 1 架“零”式战斗机冲过去，“零”式战斗机也不示弱，对着 P-40E 战斗机冲过来。2 架飞机互相对吼着冲过去，“零”式战斗机退却了。其中 1 架被击伤的“零”式战斗机拖着一缕轻烟，绕着机场盘旋。“零”式战斗机飞行员采用自杀方式冲向美国驻华空军特遣队衡阳机场，在一排停放

towards each other, but finally the Zero fighter withdrew. One Zero fighter was wounded and flew around the airport in a banking turn with a light smoke after it. The pilots of the Zero fighters flew the aircraft in a suicide way towards Hengyang Airport of the American Air Task Force in China. The Zero fighters exploded in between the P-40 fighters parking on the aircraft park, which were dummy aircraft of P-40 made of paper and rice straw.

John Ailson retired soon after the end of the Second World War. In 1962, he met a PHD with the surname of Qin who served in the same company where he worked. Qin said we met once. Qin was a boy who rescued Ailson onto the raft in Xiangjiang twenty years ago. John Ailson said later "it is really a wonder that I can come across the person in an occasion among the six hundred million Chinese people who gave me a hand when I was in great difficulties and who has become PHD and a senior engineer working in the same company of mine."

The difference between the American Air Task Force in China and the Japanese Air Force invading China in terms of the number of aircraft became greater and greater gradually. The American Air Task Force in China possessed at the time only 40 P-40 fighters and seven B-25 bombers, but had to fight against 300 operational aircraft of the Japanese troops along the half-arc route of 3220km from Hankou to Burma through Hongkong and Indochina. The only defensive way adopted by Chennault was to carry out effective attack and attack at the Japanese troops along the half-arc route with the surprise attack and maneuvering tactics, so as to prevent them from concentrating forces to launch a fatal attack on the American Air Task Force in China.

Xier Baumole, the squadron leader of the 75th Fighter Squadron of the 23rd Fighter Group of American Army 10th Air Force suffered for the most time in the summer of 1942 from malaria. Very often, he went into operations in spite of his illness. In the days when the Japanese troops launched fierce air raid at Hengyang, he once flew singly at one night to dive bomb the airport of the Japanese troops in Hankou in order to puncture the swollen arrogance of the Japanese troops. Hankou was the most defended city in China by the Japanese troops at the time. The strike at Hankou Airport by Baumole himself with a single aircraft surprised greatly the Japanese. The Japanese fighters hurried to take off to intercept Baumole's aircraft. Since then, the Japanese bombers of the Japanese troops stationing in Hankou dared not to fly to Hengyang base of the American Air Task Force in China.

John Hampsha, an American from Oregon State once serviced in Panama in the Caribbean to carry out the task of flight patrol after joining the Army Air Force. Chennault once requested General Arnold, commander of the Army Air Force to dispatch after selection a batch of pilots to China to take part in the operations. John Hampsha was one of the pilots who came to China with that batch. Hampsha was then assigned to the

在停机坪P-40战斗机中间爆炸了。可是，这些飞机却是用纸和稻草做的假的P-40战斗机。

第二次世界大战结束后，约翰·艾力逊退役了。1962年,他在自己服务的诺思勒伯有限公司见到在同一公司服务的一位姓秦的哲学博士,秦说,我们见过面。秦就是20年前，在湘江木排上救起艾力逊那个男孩子。约翰·艾力逊后来说：“当我想起在6亿中国人中间这位偶然碰到的人,他曾经在我最困难的时候帮过我的忙，今天竟成了哲学博士,成为我工作所在公司的一位高级工程师,这真是太令人惊奇了。”

美国驻华空军特遣队与侵华日本空军在数量上的差距逐步在拉大,美国驻华空军特遣队仅拥有40架P-40战斗机和7架B-25轰炸机，面对的是从汉口经香港和印度支那到缅甸的3220千米长的半弧线上日军的300架作战飞机。陈纳德惟一的防御方法就是进行有效的攻击,运用奇袭和机动战术,在半弧线上打击日军,使他们不能集中力量来给美国驻华空军特遣队以致命的打击。

美国第十航空队第23大队第75战斗机中队希尔·鲍漠勒中队长,在1942年夏天大部分时间都是患着疟疾,他经常带病坚持飞行作战。在日军发动猛烈空袭衡阳期间,为打击日军的嚣张气焰,他曾经在一天晚上单独驾机飞往汉口去俯冲轰炸日军机场。当时汉口是日军在中国防卫最严密的一个城市,鲍漠勒单机袭击汉口机场,使日本人大为震惊,赶忙起飞战机拦截。好长时间,驻汉口日军的轰炸机不敢再光顾美国驻华空军特遣队在衡阳的基地。

约翰·汉普夏是美国俄勒冈州人,参加陆军航空队后,曾经在加勒比海的巴拿马进行过飞行巡逻。陈纳德曾经要求陆军航空队总司令阿诺德上将选派一批飞行员来华参加作战,约翰·汉普夏就是随这一批的飞行员来中国的。汉普夏被分配到第23大队第75战斗机中队,中队长希尔·鲍漠勒照例要对每一位新来的飞行员进行考察。他与汉普夏一起编队飞行,汉普夏作他的僚机,跟着他飞。鲍漠

John Hampsha (third from left of people standing) took group photo with his colleagues in front of P-40 fighter.
约翰·汉普夏(站立者左三)与战友们在 P-40 战斗机前合影

75th Fighter Squadron of the 23rd Fighter Group and had to receive as usual the inspection by Xier Baumole, the squadron leader. Hampsha flew together with Baumole as his wing aircraft. Baumole made many maneuvers of great difficulty, trying to leave Hampsha far behind of him, but Hampsha followed him closely. Baumole then thought Hampsha was an excellent pilot with good flying techniques and grasped Hampsha's hand after coming down from the aircraft to show his congratulations.

Hampsha did not only have high flight techniques, but also had very good shooting techniques. He had a very good record in the operations. For twice, the Japanese Zero fighters aimed at the aircraft flown by Xier Baumole at the tail, causing Baumole in a very dangerous situation. It was Hampsha the wing aircraft of Baumole who controlled his aircraft to track, aim at and attack at the enemy's aircraft in quick actions and shot it down. Once in the air combat in Linglin of Hubei Province, a Japanese reconnaissance aircraft flew across the airport at the altitude of 2800m and dropped the leaflet saying that the Japanese would have a decisive air combat with the

勒做了许多高难度动作，想把汉普夏甩掉，可是汉普夏一直紧紧地跟着他。鲍漠勒认为汉普夏是一位技能非凡的飞行员，下了飞机鲍漠勒握着汉普夏的手向他表示祝贺。

在战斗中，汉普夏不仅飞行技术高，而且射击技术好，打得非常准。有两次中队长希尔·鲍漠勒的飞机被“零”式战斗机从尾后盯上了，情况非常危险，结果敌机被担任僚机的约翰·汉普夏给打掉了。他动作极快地操纵飞机跟踪、瞄准、射击，击落了敌机。一次在湖南零陵上空空战，日军1架侦察机在2800米高度通过机场，撒下要与美国驻华空军特遣队进行决战的传单。紧接着，后面有一队轰炸机和战斗机编队跟了过来。在高空待战的美国驻华空军特遣队正在密切注视着这些敌机。高斯少校驾驶P-40战斗机直插日军轰炸机和战斗机编队，当他正对1架敌轰炸机开火时，1架“零”式战斗机已经瞄准了他。就在这危机关头，这架“零”式战斗机突然凌空爆炸了。原来被跟踪它的汉普夏给击中了。许多队员都说，在空战中汉普夏眼快手快，击落了很多威胁队友的敌机，使队友转危为安，跟汉普夏

American Air Task Force in China. Followed the reconnaissance aircraft, came the formation of the Japanese bombers and fighters. The aircraft of the American Air Task Force in China waiting for the air combat in high altitude monitored closely the movements of these aircraft. Major Goss flew his P-40 fighter directly into the formation of the Japanese formation of bombers and fighters. However, a Zero fighter aimed at his aircraft when he was about to fire at a Japanese bomber. It was at this critical moment when that Zero fighter exploded in the air in a sudden. It was no other people but Hampsha who shot the aircraft down. Many members of the squadron later praised Hampsha that he was quick in sighting and action and had saved his colleagues from danger many times by shooting down the enemy's aircraft that endangered their aircraft. Flying together with Hampsha could have a certain sense of safety.

One day during the days when major Goss was acting as the squadron leader of the 75th Squadron, a report coming from the intelligence network said that a group of 47 Japanese Zero fighters were flying towards Hengyang Base. Major Goss headed 16 P-40 fighters to go into the air combat and they climbed to the altitude of 5500m soon after takeoff to perform air patrol. All of sudden, they found 15 Japanese Zero fighters were flying across the Hengyang Base at the altitude of 1500m. Goss doubted that there might a cheat and continued the air patrol without taking further actions against these aircraft. Later, a report from the intelligence network said that the other aircraft had flown towards other directions. Goss then gave orders to his colleagues to fire at the enemy's aircraft. There was however no outcome after a several rounds of encounters and the Japanese pilots were very clever. As Goss said "I have not achieved the success after wasting so many ammunitions." The formation was disrupted in tangled combat and pilots had to fight independently by themselves. The Japanese pilots found that they could not have the small advantages, petty gains and then flew back to Hankou. Only Hampsha shot down one enemy's aircraft in that air combat. He said that enemy's aircraft dropped to a place 1.5km north of the runway and people found the wreckages of the aircraft there. It was the 14th victory achieved by John Hampsha in his five times air combats.

On April 8th 1943, a report from the intelligence network said that eight Zero fighters were flying towards Hengyang. Major Goss headed six P-40 fighters and waited for combat in high altitude. The enemy's aircraft were above the airport and a heavy rainstorm began in a sudden. The visibility in the air was very bad and he could see nothing at all. Goss found that three Zero fighters were flying right below him and he concentrated himself to attack at that three aircraft. Just at that moment, five Zero fighters above Goss were about to attack at him. Hampsha flew his P-40 fighter to join with Goss to attack at the three Zero fighters. The five Zero fighters rear above Goss was muddled by the sudden action of the P-40 fighters and did not know what to do for quite a time. After a tangled combat, both the Americans

在一起就感到安全。

在高斯少校代理第 75 中队中队长职务期间，一天，警报网报告，日军一批 47 架“零”式战斗机正向衡阳的基地飞来。高斯少校率领 16 架 P-40 战斗机起飞迎战，他们迅速爬升到 5500 米在空中巡逻。他们发现在 1500 米有 15 架“零”式战斗机，从衡阳的基地上空飞过。高斯担心有诈没有理会这些飞机，仍在空中巡逻。后来地面情报网报告，其余敌机已向别的地方飞去，高斯才下令攻击。几个回合下来不分胜负，这些日本飞行员十分机灵，用高斯的话说，“在我耗费了许多弹药后，仍然没有获得成功。”在混战中，编队被打散了，各自为战。日本飞行员见占不到便宜，被迫退回汉口。在这次空战中，只有汉普夏 1 人击落 1 架敌机。他报告敌机掉在跑道北端 1.5 公里的地方，后来找到了敌机残骸。这是约翰·汉普夏在第 5 次空战中击落的第 14 架敌机。

1943 年 4 月 8 日，警报网报告，有 8 架“零”式战斗机向衡阳方向飞来。高斯少校率领 6 架 P-40 战斗机在高空待战。敌机已飞临机场上空，这时突然下起暴雨，空中能见度很差。高斯发现在他的右下方有 3 架“零”式战斗机，他集中注意力准备攻击那 3 架“零”式战斗机。这时，在高斯后上方的 5 架“零”式战斗机正准备向他攻击，汉普夏的 P-40 战斗机突然插进来，与高斯一起向那 3 架“零”式战斗机攻击。高斯后上方的 5 架“零”式战斗机被这突如其来的 P-40 战斗机搞懵了，一时不知所措。一阵混战后各自返回基地。高斯驾机降落后，清点人数发现少了汉普夏。当时空战在一条宽阔的河流上空，这条河流入长沙附近的湖泊。有一位飞行员说看见 1 架飞机笔直冲入湖中，很像 P-40 战斗机。另一位飞行员则说是掉入河中，并说看起来像“零”式战斗机。

正当大家争论不休时，高斯收到驻长沙地区中国军队司令官的来电。译出来的电文令人震惊：“美国飞行员落入河中，伤在胃部，肠子流出来了，速派医生来。”总算有了

and the Japanese flew their aircraft to their own bases. After landing with his aircraft, Goss counted the people and found that Hampsha had not come back. The air combat just then was carried on in the air above a wide river, which entered into the lake adjacent to Changsha. One pilot said that he saw an aircraft, which looked very like P-40 fighter dropping directly in the lake, While another pilot said that he saw an aircraft dropping into the river and that aircraft looked very much like a Zero fighter.

While they were having the heated argument, Goss received a telegraph from the commander of the Chinese troops stationing in Changsha, saying that "an American pilot fell into the river, he was wounded in the stomach and intestines had come out. Please send a doctor urgently." Everybody was relieved to learn about that, but became worried about how to bring Hampsha out of danger. Lei Spricile, surgeon of the Squadron said that he must go to bring Hampsha out of danger. Someone suggested that a people fly a P-40 fighter from Hengyang to Changsha and put doctor Spricile in the army baggage compartment and let the doctor jump out of the compartment when the aircraft was at an ultra-low altitude. Goss, the Squadron leader unexpectedly agreed to that ridiculous suggestion in desperation. The army baggage compartment could not carry person according to design and Lei Spricile had to crimp himself in the narrow compartment. Gerefen flew the P-40 fighter carrying Lei Spricile. Lightening accompanied by peals of thunder was in the sky and the rainstorm was about to come when they took off with the P-40 fighter. It was an ill omen.

Then, the second telegraph from Changsha came, saying that "the American pilot has died." Goss immediately contacted with Gerefen through radio asking him to fly homewards, but he failed to contact with him because of interference of thunders on the radio communication. Several hours passed, there was not a piece of news coming at all and there was still no news coming until the night. Everybody was anxious greatly. Some guessed that they had been at Changsha and were dealing with the aftermath of Hampsha, some guessed that they must have lost course and must have landed in a forced way at somewhere and still some guessed that they must have encountered with the Japanese Zero fighters.

In the morning of the next day, Goss, the Squadron leader sent two P-40 fighters out to search along the route for several hours, but the aircraft came back without any news at all. One man shouted out suddenly when everyone could not find the way out that "they are coming back." A P-40 fighter was taxiing on the runway and Spricile showed his head out of the army baggage compartment impatiently and waved his hand to his colleagues. Everyone began to wear a smiling face.

What had happened was really unimaginable. They lost their course completely at that night and Gerefen found a cluster of weak light on the ground suddenly when they were

汉普夏的消息了，大家都感到欣慰，但如何去营救汉普夏却犯难了。中队外科医生雷·斯普瑞茨勒表示，一定要去营救汉普夏。有人建议起飞1架P-40战斗机从衡阳飞到长沙，将雷·斯普瑞茨勒医生放在P-40战斗机的辎重舱里，超低空飞行，在汉普夏坠落的地方跳下去。情急之下，高斯中队长居然同意了这个荒唐的建议。辎重舱的设计不是载人的，雷·斯普瑞茨勒医生只能卷曲着身子呆在狭窄的辎重舱里，格瑞芬驾驶载着雷·斯普瑞茨勒医生的P-40战斗机起飞了。这时，天空雷电交加，暴风雨即将来临。这是不祥之兆……

长沙发来第二封电报："美国飞行员已死亡"。高斯中队长急忙用无线电与格瑞芬联络，要他立即返航，但无线电受雷电的干扰始终联络不上。几个小时过去了，没有一点消息；到了晚上，仍然没有任何消息。大家非常焦急，有的猜测他们已经到了长沙，正在处理汉普夏的善后事宜；有的猜测他们可能迷航了，不知迫降在什么地方；还有的猜测他们可能碰上了日本"零"式战斗机……

第二天早上，高斯中队长派出2架P-40战斗机沿航线搜寻了几小时仍无结果。大家正在一筹莫展之使，突然有人高喊："他们回来了"。1架P-40战斗机在跑道上滑行，雷·斯普瑞茨勒医生迫不及待地从辎重舱里探出了脑袋，向大家招手。大家脸上露出了笑容。

发生的事情简直是不可思议的。这天夜里，他们完全迷航了，汽油也快用完准备迫降的时候，格瑞芬突然发现地面有一簇微小的光线。因为没有电，任何一簇光线都可能意味着是一个村庄。他猜测村庄可能有电话，如果他绕着村庄盘旋，村民就会报告给警报网，基地就会知道他们迫降的地方。

当他围绕着那簇光线盘旋时，他惊异地注意到附近有长长的一连串灯在摇曳。从火焰排列的形式看，很明显是下面的中国人为他准备降落而点燃的着陆标志灯。格瑞

about out of fuel and ready for a forced landing. Any cluster of light might mean that it was a village because there was no power at that time. He guessed that there might be a telephone available in the village and if he flew the aircraft above the village in turns, the villagers would report to the intelligence network about the place where they made the forced landing.

When he made a banking turn around that cluster of light, he surprisingly found that there was a long chain of light nearby waving in the air. From the arrangement of the lights, it was obvious that the Chinese on the ground were ready for his landing by lighting the landing lights on the airport. There was not much fuel left in the aircraft flown by Gerefen. He quickly lowered the landing gears and landed in the direction of the lights in rows. What surprised him was that he landed on a flat ground and nothing unexpected happened. When he came out the cockpit, the villagers were rushing towards him. The American had no idea at all that there was an abandoned airport in this village. When watching the aircraft making turns above the village, the villagers knew that the pilot was in a dangerous situation and might be ready to make a forced landing. They suddenly had quick wits in an emergency, poured a barrel of aviation gasoline along the sides of the runway and lighted it to show the landing direction for the pilot. Gerefen and Spricile lasted a happy night with the Chinese villagers. The villagers refueled the aircraft with the emergent gasoline in the cellar and Gerefen and Spricile then flew the aircraft homewards to the base.

芬的座机油料已不多了，他赶紧放下起落架，顺着成排的火光降落了。使他感到惊奇的是，飞机降落在一块平坦的土地上，一点也没有发生意外。当他从机舱里出来时，村民们正在向他跑来。原来这个村庄有一个已被废弃的应急机场，美国人当然不知道。当村民们听到飞机在头上盘旋时，估计飞行员正处在危急之中，可能要准备迫降。他们急中生智，打开一桶航空汽油，将汽油撒在跑道边上，再点燃形成一条火光线，为飞行员指引着陆方向。格瑞芬和雷·斯普瑞茨勒医生与中国村民们度过了一个愉快的晚上。第二天早上，村民们用地窖里的应急航空汽油为飞机加满油料，格瑞芬和雷·斯普瑞茨勒便顺利返航回到基地。

2-4

Unforgettable American Pilot ——Lieutenant Robert H. Mooney

永远怀念的美国飞行员——罗伯特·H·莫尼中尉

Lt. Robert H. Mooney, a fighter pilot of American Air Task Force in China.
美国驻华空军特遣队战斗机飞行员罗伯特·H·莫尼中尉

Xiangyun is a small town in Yunnan Province and nearby there used to be Yunnanyi Airbase, where American Air Task Force in China(AATFC)stationed. On December 26, 1942, 12 Japanese bombers, covered by 20 fighter planes, took off from Canton, and launched a sudden attack on Yunnanyi Airbase. On hearing the air raid alarm, 8 P-40 fighter planes immediately took off from Yunnanyi Airport and waited in the airspace for the invaders. When flying over the base, the Japanese bombers emptied the bombs the moment they found a row of P-40 fighter planes on the airfield. In a twinkling the parking apron was on raging flames. The planes there, however, were all models made of paper and straw. The eight P-40 fighter planes smashed into the enemy bombers, but the 20 Japanese Zero fighters came for help instantly. It was indeed a bitter fight. Lt. Robert H. Mooney, a pilot of AATFC, was the first to shoot down an enemy Zero fighter. When withdrawing from the action and ready to join the formation, he found another Zero fighter ferociously heading straight for him. Fearlessly, Lt. Mooney darted at the enemy plane head-on, crashed its left wing, and sent it tumbling to the ground.

1942年12月26日，日军从广州方面起飞12架轰炸机，在20架战斗机的掩护下，突然袭击云南祥云小镇旁美国驻华空军特遣队的云南驿基地。云南驿基地的8架P-40战斗机在得到空袭警报后，立即起飞在空中待战。当日军轰炸机飞抵机场上空时，发现地面停放着一排P-40战斗机就开始投弹。机场停机坪火光冲天，当然，被炸的都是用纸和稻草做的假飞机。8架 P-40战斗机冲向敌轰炸机群，日军20架"零"式战斗立刻进行支援，空战非常激烈。空战中，美国驻华空军特遣队飞行员罗伯特·H·莫尼中尉率先击落1架敌"零"式战斗机。当莫尼退出攻击，准备重新加入编队时，1架"零"式战斗机对头向他冲来。为了不向敌人示弱，莫尼也对头冲向"零"式战斗机。一瞬间，莫尼勇敢地驾驶P-40战斗机撞向"零"式战斗机，敌机左机翼被撞断坠毁。

Xiangyun County Town, Yunnan Province, China, saved by Lt. Mooney.
被莫尼中尉拯救的中国云南祥云县城

Unfortunately, Lt. Mooney's plane was engulfed in flames, and swirled toward Xiangyun Town. At the critical moment, Lt. Mooney's only thought was to divert his plane from the town so as to avoid the catastrophic disaster that would not only kill Xiangyun people, but also ruin Yunnanyi Airbase. For the safety of Xiangyun Town that was right beneath him, Lt. Mooney did not bale out right away. Instead, he courageously piloted his burning plane and managed to bring it away from the town. Because of the fatal delay, Lt. Mooney lost the necessary altitude for baling out. After he jumped out of his plane, the parachute failed to completely open. He hurtled to the ground, and the gale blew him off course by hundreds of meters. Seriously wounded, Lt. Mooney might die at any moment. All the Xiangyun folks had seen that breathtakingly bitter air battle. As the fighter plane exploded on a hill behind the town, all the townspeople dashed out to rescue the hero, Lt. Mooney. When the dying Mooney was rushed to the operating table, Dong Jiyuan, a well-known Yunnan doctor, did his best and used all the best medicine he had on him, but failed to save him. Lt. Mooney died on the night of the same day.

莫尼驾驶的 P-40 战斗机不幸被撞起火，并失去控制向祥云县城坠落。在这紧急关头，他想到如果飞机坠落在祥云城内，将会造成灾难性的后果，还可能殃及云南驿机场。莫尼勉强操纵战机离开祥云城，在一空旷地区上空离机跳伞。由于飞机急剧下降，他失去了跳伞的最低高度，降落伞没有完全张开，下降速度很快，莫尼被重重地摔在地上。落地后，他又被大风拖拉了几百米。祥云的民众亲眼目睹了这一惊心动魄的场面，当战机在小镇后山爆炸时，祥云的民众纷纷前去抢救。莫尼被送到手术台，云南名医董济元倾其所有，全部使用最好的进口药品进行救治。莫尼终因伤势过重救治无效，当晚在祥云牺牲。

The place where Lt. Mooney received treatment.
曾经救治过莫尼中尉的地方

The entire Xiangyun Town mourned the American hero .... To show their eternal gratitude and respect for Lt. Mooney's heroic deeds, the Xiangyun people voluntarily donated money to build a monument to him. Five months later, the Monument to Lt. Robert H. Mooney of the American Air Force was completed and on the same day AATFC and the Xiangyun people jointly held a solemn ceremony to unveil the monument.

祥云民众为了永远纪念罗伯特· H ·莫尼中尉拯救祥云城的英勇壮举，自发地捐款捐物，决定为罗伯特· H ·莫尼中尉建一座纪念标。5 个月后，"美国空军莫尼中尉殉职纪念标"建成，美国驻华空军特遣队官兵与祥云民众，共同举行了纪念标落成典礼。

AATFC and the Xiangyun people jointly held a solemn ceremony to unveil the Monument to Lt. Robert H. Mooney of the American Air Force.
美国驻华空军特遣队官兵与祥云民众，共同举行莫尼中尉殉职纪念标落成典礼。

Two small towns, one in China and the other in America —— Xiangyun and North Kansas witnessed the erecting of the monuments for Lt.Robert H. Mooney, who will live forever in the memory of the peoples of the two countries...

在中国和美国的两座小城——祥云和北堪萨斯，都为莫尼中尉建立了纪念标。两座纪念标纪念的人，永远活在两城人民的心中……

Monument to Lt.Robert H. Mooney of the American Air Force in Xiangyun, China.
在中国祥云建立的莫尼中尉殉职纪念标

Monument to Lt.Robert H. Mooney of the American Air Force in North Kansas, the U.S.A..
在美国北堪萨斯建立的罗伯特·H·莫尼中尉殉职纪念标

The 5th day of the 4th lunar month, Pure Brightness, is the day traditionally observed every year as a festival by the Chinese people for worshipping at ancestral and beloved graves. On this day every year the people of Xiangyun would mournfully stand first before the monument to Lt. Mooney, paying tribute to an American martyr who is the hero in their hearts...

4月5日"清明节",是中国人祭奠祖先和亲人的日子。每年这一天,祥云人民总要先到莫尼中尉殉职纪念标前,缅怀他们心中的英雄……

Fifty years later (in 1992), Lt. Mooney's sister Ena L. Davis came to Xiangyun to see the old people who witnessed the historic episode, and their offspring and had a picture taken with them.

50年(1992年)后，莫尼中尉的妹妹埃娜·L·戴维斯来到祥云，在莫尼中尉殉职纪念标前与见证了这段历史的老人及他们的后代合影留念。

Having stayed for a while with the local people, Ena was deeply touched and chose two passages from a hymn of Rudyard Kipling, the Ballad of East and West, to Xiangyun folks.

埃娜·L·戴维斯与祥云人民共同生活一段时间后，她感慨万分，从诗人吉卜琳的一首赞美诗中节选了两段，赠与祥云人民。

Oh East is East, and West is West, and never
The twain shall meet,
Till Earth and Sky stand presently at God's
Great Judgement Seat;
But there is neither East nor West, Border,
Nor Breed, nor Birth,
When two strong men stand face to face, tho'
They come from the end of the earth!

The tumult and the shouting dies —
The captains and the kings depart —
Still stands thine ancient sacrifice,
A humble and contrite heart,
Lord God of Hosts, be with us yet,
Lest we forget!

哦！东方在东方，西方在西方，
两方不相遇，直至天和地，
站在上帝的面前，接受最后的洗礼。
可是，哪里还有东方、西方，甚至国界、种族，
两个强健的民族自地球的这方和那方，
走到一起，面对着面！

喧嚣和欢乐都已平息，
国王和首领也已逝去，
只有您的勇士啊，依然屹立，
以一颗平凡宁静的心。
全能的主啊！求您与我们共存，
为的是我们永不磨灭的记忆......
东方不再是东方，西方不再是西方！

2-5

The Augmentation of the 23rd Fighter Group

第23战斗机大队进行扩编

Col. C. L. Chennault was ready to perform a successive bombing on Hong Kong when General Clayton Bissel, the commander of the 10th Air Force, ordered him to send aircraft to bomb the Japanese army in Lashio and Myitkyina, Burma, to protect the safe Hump Flights. Although he thought that most of the Japanese had already withdrawn from those areas and it was not worthwhile covering over 1,300 Km to destroy those bases, Col. C. L. Chennault obeyed the order as he knew it was the servicemen's bounded duty to do what their superior wanted them to do.

On 25th of December 1942, Christmas Day, the Japanese aircraft attacked Yunnanyi Base, Yunnan Province where AATFC stationed. On the following day, the Japanese attempted to air raid the airbase again but they were intercepted by four P-40s over the Lancangjiang River. By a ferocious fighting in the sky, five Japanese bombers and three fighters were shot down. Nearly all the fuel in the Yunnanyi Airbase, however, had run out and they could only manage to supply very little fuel for the operation of the generators for the radios. The gasoline supply was so scarce at the Kunming base that Col. C. L. Chennault ordered that all the pilots mustn't spiral in the airspace after the combat missions.

陈纳德正准备连续轰炸香港的时候,美国陆军第十航空队司令克莱顿·比斯尔却命令他派飞机轰炸缅甸腊戌和密支那日本空军,以保证美国驼峰空运正常飞行。虽然陈纳德认为缅甸境内日本空军大多数已撤走,从桂林起飞去轰炸 1300 千米以外这些基地是得不偿失的,但军人服从命令是天职,他还是执行了比斯尔的命令。

1942 年 12 月 25 日圣诞节,日军飞机空袭美国驻华空军特遣队云南驿基地。第二天日军企图再次空袭云南驿基地时,被空袭美国驻华空军特遣队 4 架 P-40 战斗机拦截在澜沧江上空,经过一场空战,日军被击落 5 架轰炸机、3 架战斗机。云南驿基地的油料基本上全部用光了,只能够保证那里的无线电发电机工作。在昆明基地,汽油供应也非常缺乏,以至陈纳德禁止所有飞行员在完成战斗任务后在空中盘旋。

P-40 fighters of the 23rd Fighter Group were covering the Chinese Expeditionary Force in Burma.
第 23 战斗机大队的 P-40 战斗机为在缅甸的中国远征军部队提供空中支援。

At Kunming Airbase American-Chinese ground crew were repairing P-40 in close coordination, so as to keep a higher sortie generation rate of P-40 fighters in the 23rd Fighter Group.
昆明基地的中、美军地勤人员密切协作抢修 P-40E 战斗机，使第 23 战斗机大队 P-40 战斗机的出勤率一直都比较高。

In January, 1943, Lt. General Henry H. Arnold, Commander in Chief of American Air Force (on the left), meeting with Col. C. L. Chennault and other American and British army officers at Kunming Airbase.

1943 年 1 月，美国陆军航空队总司令亨利·H·阿诺德(左)中将，在昆明基地会见陈纳德和美国、英国军官。

On February 1st, 1943, at Yunnanyi Airbase, American-Chinese ground crews were rush-repairing P-40E fighters in order to get them ready to take off again.

1943 年 2 月 1 日，第 23 战斗机大队第 74 中队的中、美地勤人员在云南驿基地维护 P-40E 战斗机，为战机再次出动做好准备。

The 23rd Fighter Group's ground crews were hanging drop tanks made of bamboo and isinglass onto P-40 fighter of the 16th Fighter Squadron.
第 23 战斗机大队的地勤人员正在给第 16 战斗机中队的 P-40 战斗机挂载用竹子和鱼胶制造的副油箱

All the war materials Col. C. L. Chennault needed had to rely on the Hump Route, and some of the materials allotted to his unit often couldn't be delivered on time or reallotted to others when they arrived. Due to the lack of supplies, Col. C. L. Chennault and his men had to use locally available materials or substitutes to overcome the difficulties. They drank tea instead of coffee; they ate pork chops, stewed chicken, scrambled eggs, sautéed bean sprouts for steaks and potatoes though they preferred the latter. When the U.S. made bombs and bullets failed to arrive, they made use of the ammunition reserved in China, which were made in eleven countries, such as Russia, France, China, and Japan. When P-40 fighters were lack of aluminum drop tanks, the Chinese invented substitutive ones out of bamboo and isinglass.

陈纳德所需的物资主要靠“驼峰航线”空中运输提供，有些按计划分配给陈纳德的物资，往往不能按时运到，或者运到后又分配给了别的单位。由于供应短缺，陈纳德只好就地取材，或者用代用品。没有咖啡，就喝茶；美国人喜欢吃牛排和土豆，没有牛排和土豆，就烧猪排、煮鸡肉、炒鸡蛋、炒豆芽。美国制造的炸弹、子弹运不来，就使用中国储备的弹药。这些弹药来自 11 个国家，有苏联的、有法国的、有中国的、还有日本的……P-40 战斗机的铝制副油箱不够用，中国人就用竹子和鱼胶制造了代用品。

Col. C. L. Chennault, in order to minimize the conflicts with General Clayton Bissel, the commander of the 10th Air Force, proposed to President Roosevelt that an independent air power, under his command, should be set up for air battles in China. At the same time, President Chiang Kai-chek and Song ziwen, President of China Bank, also wrote to Mr. Roosevelt, suggesting an independent AATFC be built.

On March 3rd , 1943, Col. Chennault was promoted to major general. On March 10th, under orders, the 23rd Fighter Group of the 10th Air Force was augmented into the 14th Air Force. During the battle of nine months from July of 1942 to March of 1943, American Air Task Force in China had shot down 149 Japanese planes, and dropped more than 300 tons of bombs with the loss of 16 P-40 fighters and one B-25 bomber of their own. Whereas, Japanese fighters had only got one chance to break through the covering of the US fighters, shooting down one B-25 bomber. Major General Chennault gave the following remarks about American Air Task Force in China: It might be the smallest of American Air Forces under the command of a general over the years and, of course, it was the most fragmented unit, which didn't know well of official documents nor paid attention to social etiquettes, but it never failed to accomplish its missions whenever it went out for combat.

陈纳德为了尽量减少与陆军第十航空队司令比斯尔之间的摩擦,他建议美国总统罗斯福在中国建立一支由他指挥的独立作战的空中力量。与此同时,蒋介石与宋子文也致信罗斯福总统提出建立一支独立的驻华空军要求。

1943 年 3 月 3 日,陈纳德被晋升为少将。3 月 10 日,美国陆军第十航空队第 23 战斗机大队奉命扩编为美国陆军第十四航空队。从 1942 年 7 月至 1943 年 3 月,美国驻华空军特遣队在 9 个月的作战中,共击落敌机 149 架,投炸弹 300 余吨,自己损失 16 架P-40 战斗机和 1 架B-25 轰炸机。日本战斗机只有一次能够突破美国战斗机的掩护而击落一架 B-25 轰炸机。陈纳德对美国驻华空军特遣队的评价是:美国驻华空军特遣队也许是历年来将军级司令官指挥下的空军力量中最小的一支。当然它也是最支离破碎的,它既不习晓公文,也不考究礼节,但每当奉命出战,它却始终不辱使命。

P-40 armada of the 23rd Fighter Group was at Kunming Airbase, and their Logos had been changed into those of American Air Force.
第 23 战斗机大队在昆明基地的 P-40 战斗机机群，飞机的机徽已换成美国陆军航空队的机徽。

Lt. General Henry H. Arnold, Chief Commander of American Air Force (on the left), with Maj. General C. L. Chennault. After inspecting the 23rd Fighter Group, Mr. Arnold made the comment: Mr. Chennault was an awesome warrior, but not an excellent administrator. There was plenty of scope for Flying Tigers talents in China instead of in America.
美国陆军航空队总司令亨利·H·阿诺德(左)中将与陈纳德少将。阿诺德视察了第 23 战斗机大队后的评价是：陈纳德是一个令人敬畏的斗士，但是一个很糟糕的管理者；"飞虎队"在中国可以大有作为，在美国就不一定有所作为。

III

美国陆军第十四航空队

The 14th Air Force of U.S. Army

3-1

Establish Opertional Command

组建作战指挥部

After the declaration of war against Japan, the American government and military gradually turned to attach importance to China battlefields. In order to effectively pin down and strike relentless blows at Japanese army, on March 10th, 1943, the American government and military were determined to augment the 23rd Fighter Group of the 10th Air Force so as to set up the 14th Air Force with Major General Chennault as its commander, directly under the command of General Henry H. Arnold, the chief-commander of American Air Force. From then on, Maj. General Chennault would never receive any orders from General Bissel, Commander of the 10th Air Force, thus ending the conflicts between the two men. After its formation, the 14th Air Force received B-24 and B-25 bombers and more advanced fighter planes, such as P-51s and P-38s, therefore strengthening the offensive capability of General Chennault's Air Force. What encouraged Chennault most, however, was that he got B-24 heavy bombers he had longed for day and night, thus enabling his Flying Tigers to strike Japanese fascists more ruthlessly.

For the convenience of his work and life, the Chinese authorities supplied spacious offices and residence to General Chennault. And for Chennault, American Air Force set up a war command consisting of staff officers headed by Brigadier General Edgar Green, a graduate from West Point Military Academy. To General Chennault were also supplied a medical officer, Col. Tom Jittery and a well-known columnist, Captain Ellsop, who was a press officer in the command.

美国对日本宣战后,美国政府和军方渐渐开始重视中国战场。为了更有效地牵制和打击日军，1943 年 3 月 10 日，美国政府和军方决定将陆军第十航空队第 23 战斗机大队扩编为美国陆军第十四航空队,陈纳德任司令官。第十四航空队直接受美国陆军航空队总司令阿诺德指挥。从此陈纳德不在接受第十航空队司令比斯尔指挥,两人之间也不会再发生摩擦。第十四航空队成立后,先后得到B-24、B-25 轰炸机及 P-51、P38 等性能更优越的战斗机,使陈纳德航空队更具有进攻能力。最令陈纳德高兴的是,他终于得到了梦寐以求的 B-24 重型轰炸机，可以在中国战场狠狠地打击日本法西斯了。

为了便于陈纳德工作和生活,中国当局为他提供了宽敞的办公场所和舒适的住处。美国陆军航空队给他配备了由参谋人员组成的作战指挥部,由西点军校毕业生埃德加·格伦准将领导这个作战指挥部。为陈纳德配备了军医汤姆·吉特里上校，以及著名的报刊专栏作家爱尔索普上尉。

Up to then, the 14th Air Force was already on American active service, but the pilots and working staff were still wearing uniforms with Flying Tigers patches on them. This is newly-promoted Major General Chennault in flying-suit with a Flying Tigers patch.
美国陆军第十四航空队已经是美国正规部队，但是飞行员和工作人员服装上仍然配有“飞虎”的标志。这是已晋升少将的陈纳德身着配有“飞虎”标志的飞行服。

The 14th Air Force consisted of the 68th, 69th, 312th Wings of Air Force, four fighter groups, two bomber groups, 13 fighter squadrons, seven bomber squadrons, two reconnaissance squadrons, one night fighter squadron, one night bomber squadron, and two transport squadrons, with more than 1,000 aircraft of various types and kinds, and more than 20,000 flight and ground crewmembers in all.

The 308th Heavy Bomber Group previously under the 10th Air Force, used to station in India, and in March 1943, it was incorporated into the 14th Air Force. The 373rd, 374th, 375th, and 425th squadrons under this group then stationed respectively at Kunming Airbase, Chengjiang Airbase, and Yanggai Airbase, each equipped with five to six B-24D Bombers.

The disposition and battle command of the 14th Air Force were as follows: Brigadier General Vincent commanded the actions of the 14th Air Force in the regions to the east and the south of Kunming up to Indo-China boundary area; Brigadier General Kennedy commanded the 69th Wing of Air Force, mainly supporting the Chinese army fighting around Nujiang area; Brigadier General Landau was responsible for defending the airbases of B-29 Bombers near Chengdu and protecting the American Air Force airbases in Sichuan and Shaanxi.

In June 1943, in the light of General Chennault's proposal, a fighter pilot training center was set up in Karachi, India, for Chinese pilots' transition training. In this way, they could economize on the fuel and war materials sent by Hump Flight. China Air Force sent its pilots to receive flight training in India and, after they came back, some of the pilots formed a mixed Sino-American air regiment with part of the 14th Air Force, thus making the Chinese and American Air Forces better cooperate with each other in air battles. On November 5th, Sino-American Air Regiment was founded in Guilin, Guangxi Province, under the commander of Maj. General Chennault.

第十四航空队编有第六十八、第六十九、第三一二共3个飞行联队，4个战斗机大队、2个轰炸机大队，13个战斗机中队，7个轰炸机中队，2个侦察机中队，1个夜间战斗机中队，1个夜间轰炸机中队，2个运输机中队。装备各型飞机1000余架，空、地勤人员20000多人。

1943年3月，原驻印度的美国第十航空队第308重型轰炸机大队，划归第十四航空队。所辖的第373、374、375和425中队，分别驻防昆明、澄江、羊街等基地。每个中队装备5、6架B-24D轰炸机。

第十四航空队的兵力部署和作战指挥：文森特准将指挥昆明以东、以南直到印度支那边境地区的第十四航空队的作战行动；肯尼迪准将指挥第六十九飞行联队，主要支援在怒江附近作战的中国军队；蓝度准将负责保卫B-29轰炸机在成都附近的基地，以及四川、陕西两省境内的美国空军基地。

1943年6月，根据陈纳德的建议，在印度卡拉奇组建了战斗机飞行员训练中心，负责对中国飞行员进行改装训练。这样，可以节约经“驼峰航线”空运来的油料和军需物资。中国空军派出飞行员赴印度受训，回国后部分飞行人员与部分美国第十四航空队人员组成中美空军混合团。这样，有利于中、美空军更好地协同作战。11月5日，中美空军混合团在广西桂林成立，受陈纳德的指挥。

Battle Array of the 14th Air Force of U.S.Army
美国陆军第十四航空队战斗序列

Abbreviation（缩写）

FW	Flying Wing
HBG	Heavy Bomber Group
BS	Bomber Squadron
FG	Fighter Group
BG	Bomber Group
NFS	Night Fighter Squadron
PRS	Photo Reconnaissance Squadron
TS	Transporter Squadron
TRS	Tactical Reconnaissance Squadron

- 68th FW 第六十八飞行联队
  - 23rd FG 第 23 战斗机大队
    - 第 74 中队 74th Squadron
    - 第 75 中队 75th Squadron
    - 第 76 中队 76th Squadron
    - 第 118 战术侦察中队 118th TRS
- 69th FW 第六十九飞行联队
  - 51st FG 第 51 战斗机大队
    - 第 16 中队 16th Squadron
    - 第 25 中队 25th Squadron
    - 第 26 中队 26th Squadron
    - 第 449 中队 449th Squadron
  - 431st BG 第 431 轰炸机大队
    - 第 11 中队 11st Squadron
    - 第 22 中队 22nd Squadron
    - 第 491 中队 491st Squadron

Sino-American Air Regiment was at Guilin Airbase, Guangxi.
中美空军混合团在广西桂林的基地

In front of a P-40 fighter plane were standing Chinese Fighter Group commander, Major Yuan Jinhan (in the middle) and American Fighter Group commander, Mr. T. Alan Bennet of the Third Fighter Group, Sino-American Air Regiment.
中美空军混合团第三大队(战斗机大队)中方大队长苑金函少校(中)和美方大队长阿兰·贝内特在 P-40 战斗机前

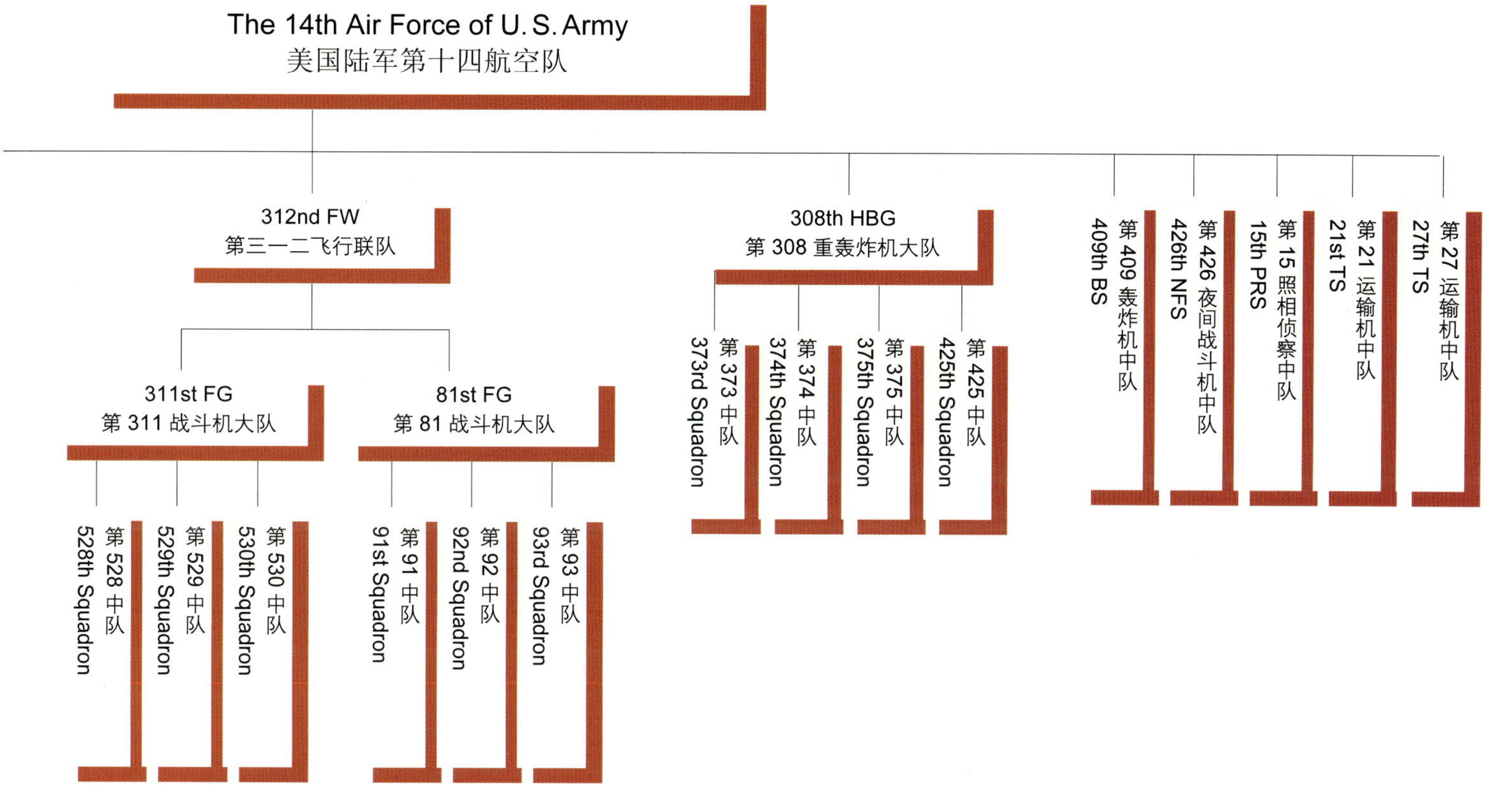

On April 24th, 1943, a pilot of the 14th Air Force shot down a Japanese Shitei-100 reconnaissance plane over Lingling Airbase. The dead pilot, Sakaetakeshi, was in Japanese Tiger air group.

1943 年 4 月 24 日，美国陆军第十四航空队的飞行员在零陵基地上空击落 1 架日军司侦 100 型侦察机。属于日军“虎”部队的飞行员小黑荣藏被击毙。

The pilots of the 14th Air Force at Lingling Airbase were examining the crashed Japanese Shitei-100 reconnaissance plane with Tiger patch on it.

美国陆军第十四航空队在零陵基地的飞行员，在查看被击落的带有“虎”部队标志的日军司侦 100 型侦察机。

3-2

Unfavorable Initial Operations

初期作战不顺利

On May 4th, 1943, the 14th Air Force dispatched 18 B-24 bombers, and 12 B-25 bombers, covered by 24 P-24 fighters. In bomber-fighter mixed formation, they flew past Laogai and along the Honghe River, to air raid Hanoi, Vietnam. And then they, in B-25A bomber and P-40 fighter formation, flew from Hanoi to make a sudden air attack on Hai-Phong. In addition, B-24Ds bombed Japanese targets in Sanya, Hainan Island, such as airports and depots. The above attacks made a serious damage to Japanese cement plant, airports, piers, refineries, and fuel depots. During those actions, only one B-24 bomber was shot by the enemy ground air-defense fire, and on the way back, the flight crews baled out above Laogai with one crewmember killed. The 14th Air Force won its first battle, but its following actions were not so favorable.

Six P-38H fighter planes arrived from India through the Hump Route in early July 1943. This type of aircraft with high ceiling was very useful for high-level air covering and reconnaissance. However, with its high fuel consumption, it was not suitable for the battlefields in China where there was a shortage of fuel. On July 24th, eight Japanese Zero fighters took off from Guangzhou and made a sudden attack on US force Lingling Airbase. During the combat, one P-38H fighter plane was shot down; later on in another combat one more was shot down, and the 3rd one was lost in bad weather. Three P-38H fighter planes were successively lost in three days.

1943 年 5 月 4 日，第十四航空队从昆明起飞 B-24 飞机 18 架、B-25 飞机 12 架，在 24 架 P-40 战斗机的掩护下，轰炸机、战斗机混合编队经老街然后沿红河而下，空袭了河内；B-25A 轰炸机和 P-40 战斗机编队，从河内又前进到海防进行突击；B-24D 轰炸机还轰炸了海南岛三亚日军的机场和仓库等目标。这次突然袭击，给日军的水泥厂、机场、码头、炼油厂和油库等设施造成了巨大破坏。在突袭行动中，仅 1 架 B-24 轰炸机被地面防空火炮击中，机组返航时在老街跳伞，1 名机组人员阵亡。第十四航空队首次作战取得成功，但是，接下来的作战却不顺利。

1943 年 7 月初，从印度经过“驼峰航线”飞来 6 架 P-38H 战斗机。这种飞机升限很高，对高空掩护和侦察很有价值。但是，它的耗油量很大，并不太适合缺油的中国战场。7 月 24 日，日军从广州出动 8 架“零”式战斗机突然袭击美军零陵基地。在战斗中 1 架 P-38H 战斗机被击落，接着在另一次战斗中又被击落 1 架，由于天气原因损失了 1 架。3 天之内连续损失 3 架 P-38H 战斗机。

B-24D Heavy Medium Bombers of the 14th Air Force. B-24D (Liberator) Heavy Medium Bomber: crewmembers: 8 ~ 10, made in American United Aircraft Co. Ltd. in 1942; length: 20.22 m; wingspan: 33.52m; height: 5.46m; power plants: 4×1200 horsepower Pratt & Whitney R-1830-43 14-cylinder air-cooled radial engines; gross weight: 27216 kg; max. air speed: 488 km/hr; ceiling: 8500m; range: 3380 km; armaments: ten 12.7mm machine guns, 4000 kg air-borne bombs.

第十四航空队装备的 B-24D 重型中程轰炸机。B-24D“解放者”重型中程轰炸机：乘员 8 至 10 人，1942 年美国联合飞机公司制造，机长 20.22 米、翼展 33.52 米、机高 5.46 米，装 4· 1200 马力普拉特-惠特尼 R-1830-43“双黄蜂”型 14 缸气冷星型发动机，全重 27216 千克，最大速度 488 千米/小时，升限 8500 米，航程 3380 千米，武器 10 挺 12.7 毫米机枪、可带炸弹 4000 千克。

A B-24D Bomber crewmember took a picture with the bomber as the background, on which shark's eyes and teeth were painted on the bomber nose to show spirits of Flying Tigers.

一个 B-24 轰炸机机组人员在 B-24D 轰炸机前合影，受“飞虎”精神的影响，B-24D 轰炸机机头也画有鲨鱼的眼睛和牙齿。

B-24D Bomber crewmembers were inspecting bombs ready to be suspended to the aircraft. The miniature bomb signs on the bomber show that this bomber had performed 24 bombing missions.

B-24D 轰炸机机组人员在检查炸弹准备挂装，从机身涂的小炸弹标志，可以看出这架 B-24D 重型轰炸机已执行过 24 次轰炸任务。

Newly equipped fighter planes of the 14th Air Force. P-38H Lightning fighter planes: crewmember: one; manufactured by US Lockheed Martin Company in 1942; length: 11.53m; wingspan: 15.85 m; height: 2.99m; equipped with 2x1250 horsepower Allison V-1710-49V 12-cylinder liquid-cooled engines; gross weight: 9065 kg; max. air speed: 636 km/h; ceiling: 11880 m; max. range: 2000 km. Armaments: 1x20-mm cannon, 4x12.7 mm machine guns, and 900 kg bombs. This was a P-38H fighter plane still with the patch of US Army Air Force in 1942 on it, and its new patch had not yet been painted.

第十四航空队新装备的战斗机。P-38H“闪电”战斗机：乘员 1 人，1942 年美国洛克希德飞机公司制造，机长 11.53 米、翼展 15.85 米、机高 2.99 米，装 2· 1250 马力艾利逊 V-1710-49V 型 12 缸液冷发动机，全重 9065 千克，最大速度 636 千米/小时，升限 11880 米，航程 2000 千米，武器 1 门 20 毫米机炮、4 挺 12.7 毫米机枪，可载 900 千克炸弹。这是 1 架喷有 1942 年美国陆军航空队机徽的 P-38H，还来不及喷新的机徽。

In late-July, Japanese force dispatched its bombers and fighters from Guangzhou and Hankou, air raiding the airports of the Chinese and American air forces along the Peking-Kwangchow Railway Line. The airbases of the 14th Air Force in Hengyang, Lingling and Guilin successively suffered Japanese sudden attacks.

On the morning of August 21st, the 374th and 375th Bomber Squadrons of Kunming Airbase dispatched 14 B-24D bombers to air raid Hangzhou. According to the schedule, the bombers group would, over Hengyang , meet the covering P-40 fighter group, forming a combat formation. Supposed to escort the bomber group, Colonel Bruce Holloway, commander of the 23rd Fighter Group sent his P-40 fighters to attack another group of Japanese planes. When the battle was over, the P-40s returned to the airbase, and after getting refueled and reloaded, took off again for the escort mission. The B-24D bombers had

7 月下旬，日军分别从广州和汉口起飞轰炸机和战斗机，对京广线铁路沿线上的中、美空军机场进行袭击。第十四航空队在衡阳、零陵、桂林地基地也连续遭到日本空军的突袭。

8 月 21 日上午，昆明基地第 374 和第 375 轰炸机中队，出动 14 架 B-24D 轰炸机轰炸杭州。按计划轰炸机编队要与担任护航任务的 P-40 战斗机编队，在衡阳上空汇合。担任护航任务的第 23 战斗机大队大队长布鲁斯·霍洛韦上校，将属下的 P-40 战斗机派出参加攻击另一队日军飞机，待战斗结束后，P-40 战斗机返回基地加油、加弹后，再去执行为轰炸机编队的护航任务。B-24D 轰炸机已习惯于在没有战斗机护航的情况下战斗出动，他们没有经衡阳，而是直飞汉口，再从汉口直飞杭州。14 架 B-24D 轰炸机编队在汉口遇到日军 80 架“零”式战斗机的围攻，由于

Chinese and American ground crewmen studying the armament structure and practicing loading and unloading by referring to the structural diagram.
中、美地勤人员在熟悉 P-38H 的军械构造，看着结构图在练习装、退子弹。

Since the 14th Air Force was equipped with a new type of plane, Gen.Chennault arranged for air surveillance operators of the warning network to visit the new planes at US airbases, in order to get them familiar with the new plane. This was air surveillance operators visiting P38-H fighter plane.
由于第十四航空队装备了新的机种，为了使对空监视员熟悉美军新机种的特点，陈纳德组织警报网的对空监视员到美军基地参观新机种。这是对空监视员在参观 P-38H 战斗机。

When the two damaged B-24Ds returned to the airbase, comrades in arms came to greet and comfort them, and correspondents came to have an interview. The scene was moving and sorrowful for after all there were 50 of them killed, injured or missing.
第 425 中队 2 架受伤 B-24D 轰炸机返回基地后，战友们前去慰问、记者前去采访，场面既热闹又悲伤，毕竟有 50 人阵亡、受伤或失踪。

got used to act without fighters' escort, they flew directly to Hangzhou via Hankou instead of Hengyang. The 14 B-24D bombers suffered besiegement by 80 Japanese Zero fighters in Hankou without fighters' escort. The bombers could only fight back with their own cannons and guns. In half an hour's fierce air battle, two US B-24D bombers were shot down (one of them was the leader plane piloted by Major Bruce Beet, squadron leader), 11 B-24D bombers were damaged, one of which was severely damaged and made a force landing in Lingling, with 11 crewmembers killed and 4 injured in this combat.

On the afternoon of August 21st, the 373rd and 425th Bomber Squadrons at the Kunming Airbase respectively dispatched seven B-24D bombers to Hankou for revenge. On their way, the 373rd Squadron got lost and returned to the Airbase due to bad weather. The 425th Bomber Squadron had to go alone and their seven B-24Ds bombed Hankou Airport, bringing a big loss to the Japanese. However, the B-24D group were attacked and fired by 40 Zero fighters and air defense artillery. In the 45-minute combat, four B-24Ds were shot down, and another one crashed on its way back. So, of the B-24D bombers of the seven of the 425th Squadron, only two injured ones came back to Kunming Airbase. Of the 70 crewmembers, 50 were killed, injured or missing.

These two lessons made the bomber crewmembers deeply aware that what Gen.Chennault said was correct: "No bombers should be dispatched for action with ease without fighters' escort."

Japanese pilots gradually found out the weak points of Col. C. L. Chennault's pilots through the combats. They adopted a new set of tactic: Japanese pilots raced to control the commanding point and waited at high altitude for fight (Zero fighters' ceiling was higher than P-40H's). When US P-40s initiated climbing to intercept the Japanese planes, the Zeros dived from the top to attack the P-40s. The Japanese pilots only did one diving attack once, and then went back to their Airbase immediately. This tactic resulted in a good success, and three US P-40s were successively lost in a few days.

From July to August 1943, the US 14th Air Force coordinated with ground force and launched fierce offensives against Japanese Air Force in Hunan and Guangxi. Japanese employed their upgraded Zero fighters for operation. In two months, Japanese lost 53 planes and the 14th Air Force 27.

没有战斗机护航，仅仅依靠轰炸机自身的火炮反击。经过半个小时激烈地空战，美军被击落 2 架 B-24D 轰炸机（其中 1 架带队长机，中队长布鲁斯·比特少校），被击伤 11 架 B-24D 轰炸机，其中 1 架受重伤的 B-24D 轰炸机在零陵迫降；11 人阵亡，4 人受伤。

8 月 21 日下午，昆明基地第 373 和第 425 轰炸机中队，分别出动 7 架 B-24D 轰炸机前往汉口报仇。第 373 中队在途中，因天气不好迷航返回基地，第 425 轰炸机中队只好孤军前往。7 架 B-24D 轰炸机轰炸了汉口机场，日军受到较大损失。但是，B-24D 轰炸机队遭到 40 架“零”式战斗机的攻击和地面防空火炮的猛烈射击。经过 45 分钟的战斗，有 4 架 B-24D 轰炸机被击落，1 架在返航的途中坠毁。第 425 中队的 7 架 B-24D 轰炸机中，仅有 2 架受伤 B-24D 轰炸机回到昆明基地。机组成员共 70 人，有 50 人阵亡、受伤或失踪。

经过这两次挫折，轰炸机机组人员深刻认识到了陈纳德曾经讲过的“没有战斗机护航，轰炸机不要轻易出动”的正确性。

日军飞行员在交战中也逐渐摸索到了陈纳德的飞行员作战的弱点。日本人对美国人使用了一套新的战术：日军飞行员驾驶“零”式战斗机编队飞临第十四航空队基地附近上空，在高空（“零”式战斗机的升限比 P-40 战斗机要高）等待，待美国人驾驶 P-40 战斗机开始爬高准备拦截日军飞机时，“零”式战斗机从高空俯冲下来，攻击 P-40 战斗机。日军飞行员只俯冲攻击 1 次，攻击后立即返回基地。日军飞行员的这一战术还真奏效，几天中连续击落美国人 3 架 P-40 战斗机。

1943 年 7 月至 8 月，美国陆军第十四航空队协同地面部队在湖南、广西两省，向日本空军发动了猛烈进攻，日军使用最新改进型“零”式战斗机作战。在两个月内，日军损失 53 架飞机，第十四航空队损失 27 架飞机。

P-51 Mustang fighter plane was a well known fighter in WWII. The 14th Air Force began to be equipped with P-51A, -B, -C and -D gradually from the second half of 1943. P51-D was mostly used since 1944.

P-51“野马”战斗机是第二次世界大战中非常有名的战斗机。美国陆军第十四航空队从 1943 年下半年起，先后陆续装备 P-51A、B、C、D 等型战斗机。从 1944 年开始使用 P-51D 战斗机比较多。

P-51A Mustang fighter plane: crewmember: one; manufactured by US North American Company in 1943. It was 9.83 m in length, 11.28 m in wingspan, 2.65 m in height, and was equipped with 1x1200 horsepower Ellison V-1710-81V 12-cylinder liquid-cooled engine, with gross weight 3992 kg., max. airspeed 628 km/h, ceiling 9550 m, and max range 1200 km. It carried 4x12.7 mm machine guns and 454 kg bombs.

P-51A“野马”战斗机：乘员 1 人，1943 年美国北美航空公司制造，机长 9.83 米、翼展 11.28 米、机高 2.65 米，装 1200 马力艾利逊 V-1710-81V 型 12 缸液冷发动机，全重 3992 千克，最大速度 628 千米/小时，升限 9550 米，航程 1200 千米，武器 4 挺 12.7 毫米机枪，可载 454 千克炸弹。

P-51D Mustang fighter plane: crewmember: one; manufactured by US North American Company in 1944. It had a 9.83 m length, 11.28 m wingspan, 4.20 m height, and its power plant was 1x1510 horsepower Parked V-1650-7 12-cylinder liquid-cooled engine, with gross weight 5262 kg, max. air speed 703 km/h, ceiling 12771 m, and max. range 1530 km. It was equipped with 6x12.7 mm machine guns and could carry 907 kg bombs.

P-51D“野马”战斗机：乘员 1 人，1944 年美国北美航空公司制造，机长 9.83 米、翼展 11.28 米、机高 4.20 米，装 1510 马力帕卡德 V-1650-7 型 12 缸液冷发动机，全重 5262 千克，最大速度 703 千米/小时，升限 12771 米，航程 1530 千米，武器 6 挺 12.7 毫米机枪，可载 907 千克炸弹。

Ground crew were loading bullets and hanging bombs onto a P-51D fighter plane, 1780 bullets needed to be loaded for six 12.7 mm machine guns each time and two hangers could carry a 450 kg bomb each.
地勤人员在为 P-51D 战斗机装子弹、挂炸弹，6 挺 12.7 毫米机枪一次需要装 1780 发子弹，2 个挂架可挂载 2 枚各为 450 千克的炸弹。

In 1995, in order to celebrate the 50th anniversary of victory over Japanese fascists, airplane collectors and aviation fans piloted B-25 bomber and P-51 fighter again in the blue sky. This is one B-25 bomber and one TP-51 Fighter (double-seat trainer, a correspondent seated at the back) simulating the combat formation 50 years ago.
1995 年为庆祝战胜日本法西斯 50 周年，飞机收藏家和航空爱好者将 B-25 轰炸机和 P-51 战斗机重新飞上蓝天。这是 1 架 B-25 轰炸机和 1 架 TP-51（双座教练型，后座是名记者）战斗机在模拟当年编队飞行。

The 426th Night Fighter Squadron of the 14th Air Force had eight P-61B night fighters, which were specially used to deal with Japanese fighters and bombers coming at night.

第十四航空队第426夜间战斗机中队装备8架P-61B的夜间战斗机，专门用于对付夜间来袭的日军战斗机和轰炸机。

P-61B Black Widow fighter plane: crewmember:3, manufacturer: U.S. Northrop Aircraft Company Ltd. in 1944. It had a 15.11 m length, 20.11 m wingspan, and 4.47 m height, and was equipped with 2x2,000 horsepower Pratt-Whiney R-2,800-65 18-cylinder air-cooled engines with gross weight 17,200 kg, max. air speed 589 km/h, ceiling 10,100 m, and max. range 4,830 km. It carried 4x 20mm cannons, 4x 12.7- mm machine guns and could carry 2,900 kg bombs.

P-61B"黑寡妇"战斗机：乘员3人，1944年美国诺斯罗普飞机股份有限公司制造，机长15.11米、翼展20.11米、机高4.47米，装2· 2000马力普拉特-惠特尼R-2800-65"双黄蜂"型18缸气冷发动机，全重17200千克，最大速度589千米/小时，升限10100米，航程4830千米，武器4门20毫米机炮、4挺12.7毫米机枪，可载2900千克炸弹。

The P-61Bs of the 426th Night Combat Squadron, which were responsible for defending the B-29 bomber airbases near Chengdu, were painted black for convenience of night operation.

担任保卫成都附近B-29轰炸机基地的第426夜间战斗机中队的P-61B，为适应夜间防空作战整个飞机涂成黑色。

Japanese Air Force began to use improved Mitsubishi A6M5 Zero fighters from the second half of 1943.

从 1943 年下半年起，日本空军开始使用改进型三菱 A6M5“零”式战斗机。

Mitsubishi A6M5 Zero fighters: crewmember: one; manufactured by Japanese Mitsubishi Heavy Industries Company Ltd. in 1943. It had a 9.20 m length, 11.00 m wingspan and 3.55 m height and was equipped with an 1130 horsepower NKIF-21 14-cylinder air-cooled radial engine with gross weight 2738 kg, max. air speed 564 km/h, ceiling 11740 m, and max. range 1920 km. It carried 2x20mm cannons and 2x12.7 mm machine guns and could carry 120 kg bombs.

三菱 A6M5“零”式战斗机：乘员 1 人，1943 年日本三菱重工业公司制造，机长 9.20 米、翼展 11.00 米、机高 3.55 米，装 1130 马力中岛 NK1F“荣”21 型 14 缸气冷星型发动机，全重 2738 千克，最大速度 564 千米/小时，升限 11740 米，航程 1920 千米，武器 2 门 20 毫米机炮、2 挺 13 毫米机枪、120 千克炸弹。

A-26B Invader attack plane held 3 crewmembers, manufactured by U.S. Douglas Company in 1944. It had a 15.45 m length, 21.33 m wingspan and 5.64m height, carried 2x2000 horsepower Pratt-Whiney R-2800-72 18-cylinder air-cooled radial engines with gross weight 15876 kg, max. speed 571km/h, ceiling 9600 m, max. range 2900 km. It carried 10x12.7mm machine guns and could carry 1815 kg bombs.

A-26B“侵略者”攻击机：乘员 3 人，1944 年美国道格拉斯飞机公司制造，机长 15.45 米、翼展 21.33 米、机高 5.64 米，装 2· 2000 马力普拉特-惠特尼 R-2800-27 “双黄蜂” 型 18 缸气冷星型发动机，全重 15876 千克，最大速度 571 千米/小时，升限 9600 米，航程 2900 千米，武器 10 挺 12.7 毫米机枪，可载 1815 千克炸弹。

During the Japanese air raid on Sino-American Liangshan Airbase, Chuck Tucker, a pilot of the 23rd Fighter Group of the 14th Air Force, was killed.
日军突然袭击中、美空军在四川的梁山基地，美军第十四航空队第 23 战斗机大队飞行员恰克·塔克不幸牺牲。

On June 6,1943, eight Japanese Nine Nine Bombers of the 90th Air Group made a sudden air raid on Sino-American Liangshan Airbase, Sichuan, resulting in damage to more than 20 Sino-American P-40 fighter planes.
1943 年 6 月 6 日，日军第 90 战队 8 架“九九”式轰炸机突然袭击中、美空军四川梁山基地，共炸毁中、美空军 20 余架 P-40 战斗机。

3-3

Gradual Seizure of Theater Initiative

逐步掌握战场主动权

The main purpose of the American Volunteer Group (A.V.G.) and the American Air Task Force in China was to defend important objects and strategic points and support ground forces in operation. The 14th Air Force was mainly to assist the ground forces to attack Japanese initiatively. In July and August, 1943, the 14th Air Force suffered some setbacks in actions. They drew lessons from the setbacks, summed up experience and adopted some active measures. At the same time, they got P-51 fighter planes with better performance. In the following combats, they gradually gained the initiative in operations and achieved much better results.

On November 25th, 1943, 12 B-25 bombers, led by Tuckers Hill covered by eight P-38 and seven P-51 fighters, flew over Taiwan Strait at low altitude and made a sudden attack on Xinzhu Airport in Taiwan. The bombers dropped bombs and fighters fired at ground targets with cannons and guns, destroying more than 30 Japanese planes on the ground and shooting down 6 enemy planes in the air. On December 1st, thirteen B-25 bombers, covered by twenty-four P-40s and eight P-51s, air raided Japanese navy airbases in Hong Kong and Kowloon, sinking a large freighter ship and damaging many other ships. Japanese suffered a big loss. On December 24th, twenty-eight B-24 Bombers of the 308th bomber Group of the 14th Air Force, escorted by twenty-four P-40s and six P-51s, bombed Tianhe Airport of Guangzhou, a very important Japanese airbase, destroying six planes on the ground and shooting down three in the air.

美国志愿航空队、美国驻华空军特遣队的作战行动主要是保卫重要目标、战略要地，以及支援地面部队作战；美国陆军第十四航空队则主要是配合地面部队主动向日军发起进攻。1943 年 7、8 两个月，第十四航空队作战不顺利。在认真总结经验教训的基础上，采取了一些积极措施。同时，增加了像 P-51 这样性能优秀的战斗机。在随后的战斗中，逐步掌握战场主动权，取得了比较好的战果。

1943 年 11 月 25 日，由塔克斯·希尔率领 12 架 B-25 轰炸机，在 8 架 P-38 和 7 架 P-51 战斗机的掩护下，低空飞越台湾海峡，突然空袭台湾新竹机场，轰炸机投弹轰炸，战斗机利用航炮、机枪对地扫射，炸毁、击毁日军地面飞机 30 余架，空中击落敌机 6 架。12 月 1 日，13 架 B-25 轰炸机在 24 架 P-40 和 8 架 P-51 战斗机掩护下空袭香港及九龙日军海军基地，炸沉大型货船 1 艘、炸伤多艘，给日军造成重大损失。12 月 24 日，第十四航空队第 308 轰炸机大队的 28 架 B-24 轰炸机，在 24 架 P-40 和 6 架 P-51 战斗机的掩护下空袭了日军重要空军基地——广州天河机场，炸毁敌机 6 架，空战中击落敌机 3 架。

Bomber and Fighter formation of the 14th Air Force flying over Taiwan Strait at a low altitude to bomb a railway bridge controlled by Japanese in Taiwan.
第十四航空队的轰炸机、战斗机混合编队低空飞越台湾海峡，轰炸台湾日军控制的铁路桥。

John Hurst of the 14th Air Force, who shot down two enemy planes, receiving congratulations from others.
第十四航空队的约翰·赫尔斯特击落 2 架敌机，大家向他祝贺。

Hearing the air alarm, members of the 539th Squadron of the 311th Fighter Group rushing to their P-40E fighter planes.
听到警报声，第 311 战斗机大队第 539 中队的队员们快速奔向 P-40E 战斗机。

In April 1944, the Japanese launched an operation, attempting to open a continent communication line, so that north-eastern China could be linked with Singapore. In April and May, the Japanese started to wage a fierce attacks on Chinese armed forces stationed in Henan, Hunan and other places. The 14th Air Force was then ordered to send two hundred fighters to defend the B-29 bomber airbase close to Chengdu and 150 planes to support Gen. Stilwell who would launch attacks on the Japanese in Nujiang Area. So, there were only 90 planes left for Gen. Chennault to send to Henan and Hunan for operation.

1944 年 4 月，日军为使从中国东北到新加坡的日军连成一片，发动了打通大陆交通线的作战行动。4 月和 5 月，日军开始向河南、湖南等地的中国军队发动猛烈进攻。这时，第十四航空队奉命派 200 架战斗机执行保卫成都附近 B-29 轰炸机基地的任务，同时派 150 架飞机去支援史迪威在怒江对日军将发动的攻势。这样，陈纳德只有 90 架飞机可以派往河南、湖南等战场作战。

6 月，日本人发现美国轰炸机装有机载雷达，感到十分震惊，要求日本军舰夜间航行实行灯火管制。一天，第 308 轰炸机大队第 425 中队由杰伊·列文驾驶的 B-24D 轰炸

In June, the Japanese was shocked to find that the American bombers had been equipped with airborne radar, and ordered that Japanese warships conduct light control at night. One day, Joy Levin from the 425th Squadron of the 308th Bomber Group piloted his B-24D bomber from the advanced airport of Liuzhou to Hainan Island. When approaching Hainan Island, he saw a big pulse signal on the radar screen, but he didn't know what the target was. From the dark sky, John Hitter, the bombardier, dropped two 450kg time bombs which hit the target. In the sound of explosion, the Japanese lighted up and fired toward the air. The B-24D bomber reentered and bombed it again. The target got on fire and sank finally. It turned out later that the sunken target was a Nakano cruiser of the Japanese navy. Under the strong attacks by Japanese ground force, the 14th Air Force was forced to withdraw from Hengyang Airport and moved to Lingling Airbase. Hengyang was lost on August 8th. On October 11th, the Japanese occupied Liuzhou Airbase of the 14th Air Force. Gen. Chennault could then only rely on Kunming Airbase and a few other airbases for operation.

On August 8th, Hengyang of Hunan fell, which formed a direct threat to the 14th Air Force airbases in Kunming and Guilin. If the whole South China was occupied by the Japanese, the air warning network that Gen. Chennault had set up in

机，从柳州前进机场起飞飞向海南岛。接近海南岛时，从雷达显示器的荧光屏上看到一个大脉冲信号，但不清楚是什么目标。在漆黑的夜空中，轰炸员约翰·希特尔向目标投下2枚450千克重定时炸弹，命中目标。在爆炸声中，日本人开灯并对空射击。B-24D 轰炸机再次进入投弹轰炸，目标已开始燃烧，最后沉没了。事后查明，炸沉的是1艘日本海军的永野级巡洋舰。在日军地面部队强大的攻势下，6月26日，第十四航空队的部队被迫撤出衡阳机场，迁往零凌基地。8月8日衡阳被日军攻陷。10月11日，日军又占领了第十四航空队在柳州的基地，陈纳德只能依托昆明等少数几个基地坚持作战。

8月8日，湖南衡阳失陷，直接威胁到第十四航空队在昆明的基地和广西桂林机场。如果华南地区全部被日军占领，陈纳德多年来在中国建立的空中警报网络系统将遭到破坏。为了保卫昆明基地和广西桂林机场，先后出动轰炸机、战斗机，共5287架次，投弹1164吨，对地攻击使用子弹110万发；在出动的150架飞机中，损失43架。炸毁、击落敌机114架，炸毁、击毁敌卡车595辆、运输船1000余艘，敌军伤亡13000余人。

10月，美国海军航空母舰出动1000架飞机对日军作战。第十四航空队积极配合美海军作战，在不到半年时间

P-51B Fighter planes of the 14th Air Force parking at the advanced airport in Laohekou, Hubei Province; a group of civil workers pulling stone rollers to roll the emergency runway smooth.
美国陆军第十四航空队在湖北老河口前进机场停放的P-51B战斗机。一群民工拉着大石滚在碾压备用起降场地。

On August 13th, 1944, B-25H bombers of the 14th Air Force bombed the Japanese in Wan Tup, Burma , to support Chinese and British ground forces operation in Burma.
1944 年 8 月 13 日，第十四航空队 B-25H 轰炸机在缅甸万托地区轰炸日军，支援在缅甸的中国和英国地面部队作战。

In November 1944, the Japanese bombed the 14th Air Force's Lijiazhen Airbase near Guilin. The runway was totally damaged and out of use.
1944 年 11 月，日军轰炸机轰炸了第十四航空队在桂林附近的李家镇基地，跑道完全被破坏不能使用。

On the morning of March 10th, 1945, B-25H bombers of Sino-US Air Force bombing the Japanese-controlled the Yellow River Iron Bridge.
1945 年 3 月 10 日上午，中、美空军的 B-25H 轰炸机轰炸日军占领的黄河大铁桥。

China for many years would be destroyed completely. In order to defend Kunming Airbase and Guilin Airport, bombers and fighters made 5287 flights sorties in total, 1164 tons of bombs were dropped and 1.1 million bullets were fired in air-to-ground operations of the 150 actions of the 14th Air Force, 43 planes were lost, with 114 enemy planes were shot down or destroyed, 595 enemy vehicles and more than 1000 transport ships destroyed, and more than 13,000 enemy troop killed or wounded.

In October, US Navy dispatched one thousand planes from aircraft carriers to fight against the Japanese. The 14th Air Force actively joined the Navy in the operation. They destroyed more than 500 Japanese planes and 40 warships in less than 6 months. On December 18th, 77 US B-29 bombers dispatched in 7 batches to bomb Japanese-occupied Hankou, causing the important airbase of the Japanese Air Force in China almost completely destroyed.

On the morning of March 10th, 1945, Chinese and American pilots of Sino-US Air Force Regiment carried out a hard and dangerous "death flight task"- bombing the Japanese-controlled the Yellow River Iron Bridge. There were two hundred 75mm air-defense artillery around the bridge, forming a tight fire net within a radius of 2000 meters. Two B-25H bombers dove from high altitude and missed the target for the first time. They approached again at a low level, receiving heavy shellfire from the Japanese. No.1 Bomber dropped six 227 kg bombs, all hitting the target. The bridge was broken. No.2 Bomber was shot down before approaching the target, and all the nine crewmembers on board died. No.1 Bomber came back to Xi'an Airbase with difficulties with 120 wounds on the plane.

In 1945, the 14th Air Force assisted the Chinese forces throughout the battle field in China and launched attacks, in cooperation with US Navy, on Japanese airbases in Taiwan, Hong Kong and the Philippines. The 14th Air Force had then gained the initiative and air domination through the battlefield in China.

内使日军损失飞机 500 多架，舰船 40 多艘。12 月 18 日，美军 77 架 B-29 轰炸机分 7 批对日军占领的汉口进行轰炸，使日本空军在中国的重要基地几乎完全被摧毁。

1945 年 3 月 10 日上午，中美空军混合团的中、美空军飞行员共同进行一项既艰巨又危险的“死亡飞行任务”——轰炸日军占领的黄河大铁桥。铁桥周围有 200 门 75 毫米高炮防卫，形成一个半径 2000 米的严密火网。2 架 B-25H 轰炸机第一次高空进入投弹未命中目标，第二次改为低空进入，随即遭到日军防空炮火的猛烈抗击。1 号机投下 6 枚 227 千克炸弹全部命中目标，铁桥被炸断；2 号机还未进入目标就被击落，机上 9 人全部牺牲。1 号机带着 120 处伤痕勉强飞回了西安基地。

在 1945 年，第十四航空队在整个中国战场协同中国军队作战，并配合美海军袭击日本在台湾、香港、菲律宾等基地。这时，第十四航空队已在中国战场取得主动权和制空权。

3-4

B-29 Strategic Bomber Team

B-29战略轰炸机队

In order to satisfy the requirement of Pacific Theater, B-29 long-distance super heavy bomber was developed as an emergency measure, which was designated Martehen Plan. The US government believed that a strategic army bomber team should be set up, named the 20th Bomber Team, directly commanded by Joint Chiefs of Staff, with General Arnold, the commander in chief of US Army Air Force, as its executive agent. On April 10th, 1944, the 20th Bomber Team was established, whose B-29 bomber group permanently stationed in Calcutta, India, for which General Wolfe took the concrete responsibility. The main task of the 20th Bomber Team was to conduct strategic bombing on the important targets in the territory of Japan (to destroy fundamental war material production bases, such as iron and steel plants) and in the theaters in China, India and Burma and the Pacific theater. Chengdu, China was selected as the advanced airbase of the B-29 bomber team. The 14th Air Force led by Gen. Chennault was in charge of dispatching fighter planes to defend the airbase, and therefore, airfields near Chengdu were built and logistic support was provided.

In order to ensure safe takeoff and landing of B-29 long-range heavy bombers, the 14th Air Force employed a great number of laborers, with the most primitive tools and ways, and sometimes even sent soldiers to build or extend five airfields in the areas around Chengdu, China, such as Phoenix Mount, Shuangliu, Xinjin, Pengshan, and Guanghan.

为了太平洋战场的需要,美国紧急研制超远程重型轰炸机 B-29(称为“马特亨”计划)。美国政府认为,“建立一支战略性的陆军轰炸机队，命名为第 20 轰炸机队。直接由参谋长联席会议指挥,由陆军航空队总司令阿诺德上将任执行代理。” 1944 年 4 月 10 日，第 20 轰炸机队成立。B-29 轰炸机队常驻基地在印度的加尔各答,由沃尔夫将军具体负责。第 20 轰炸机队的任务:对日本本土(摧毁基本战争物资的生产,如钢铁生产基地等),中、缅、印战区和太平洋战区的重要目标实施战略轰炸。中国成都作为 B-29 轰炸机队的前进基地。由陈纳德的第十四航空队负责派出战斗机保护 B-29 轰炸机队基地，在成都附近修建机场及提供后勤保障。

为了保障 B-29 远程重型轰炸机安全起降，由第十四航空队雇用大量民工采用最原始的方法,有时甚至动用部队士兵,在中国成都附近的凤凰山、双流、新津、彭山、广汉等地新建或扩建了 5 个机场。

B-29 (Super Fortress) Long-Range Heavy Bomber: crewmembers: 10, made in Boeing Company, U.S.A., in 1944; length: 30.18m; wingspan: 43.05m; height: 9.02m; with 4×2200 horsepower Wright R-3350-57 Cyclone 18-cylinder air-cooled radial engines; gross weight: 63958 kg; maximum airspeed: 576 km/hr; ceiling: 9700 m; range: 6600 km; weapons: one 20mm cannon; 10 12.7mm machine guns; 9090 kg airborne bombs.

B-29“超级保垒”远程重型轰炸机：乘员 10 人，1944 年美国波音飞机公司制造，机长 30.18 米、翼展 43.05 米、机高 9.02 米，装 4· 2200 马力莱特 R-3350-57“塞克隆”型 18 缸气冷星型发动机，全重 63958 千克，最大速度 576 千米/小时，升限 9700 米，航程 6600 千米，武器 1 门 20 毫米机炮、10 挺 12.7 毫米机枪，可带炸弹 9090 千克。

Thousands upon thousands of laborers shouldering soil and stones to the construction site.
成千上万的民工用肩挑的方式搬运土方和石料。

Tens of laborers had to haul a large stoneroller, running to and fro, to roll runway surface smooth because it was too difficult to carry a bulldozer over the Hump.
由于没有推土机可以运过“驼峰”，只能用几十名民工拉着大石滚不断的来回碾压，压平机场跑道。

The laborers of Sichuan Province were building Xinjin airfield. No sooner had a B-29 bomber taken off than they began pulling a stoneroller to press the runway.
四川民工在修建新津机场，一架B-29轰炸机刚起飞，民工们就拉着大石滚碾压道面。

At a construction site laborers scrapping stones with hammers, where elders and women usually did such job.
民工在工地上用锤子敲碎石头，这种工作通常由老人和妇女来完成。

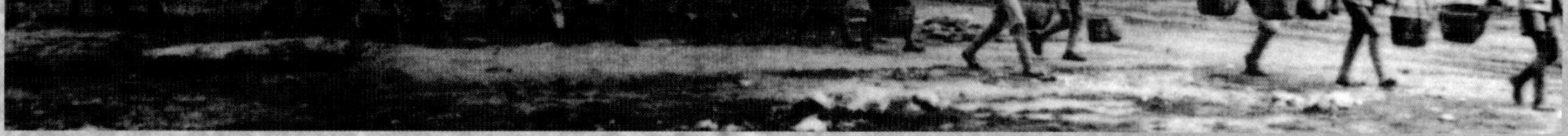

As soon as the runway at advanced airfield near Chengdu for B-29 bombers was completed, B-29 bombers entered and made their base there. Because of being short of labor power, the Chinese military had to employ soldiers to help build the transition strip at Shuangliu Airfield, Chengdu.

成都附近 B-29 轰炸机前进机场的跑道完成后 B-29 轰炸机就进驻，由于民工不够用，中国军方不得不派遣士兵来帮助修建成都双流机场的联络道。

On the morning of June 5th, 1944, 112 B-29 bombers from Calcutta, India, performed a 3,200 km round-trip mission, bombing Marcasum Railway Vehicle Factory in Bangkok, Thailand. One B-29 bomber piloted by the captain, Major John Keller, crashed soon after it took off from Charkulia Airport of Calcutta, with all the flight crew on board killed except one. Shortly after taking off, 14 of the bombers had to fly home due to mechanical failures. From 8,200 m height, B-29s dropped bombs at the target by means of radar sight. Although the enemy antiaircraft fire was very fierce, the bombers flew too high to be shot. Only a few enemy fighter planes attempted to intercept the bombers, but none of them succeeded because of the violent gunfire of the B-29s. The first bombing action of B-29 bombers turned out to be mediocre.

Rainy season was coming, which tortured them more ruthlessly than the Japanese. During the period B-29 bombers made a ferry flight training from Calcutta Base, India, to Kunming Airport, China, and then back to Calcutta Base after refueling at Kunming Airport. One bomber crashed at DamDam field shortly after taking off and three others fell into the Bay of Bengal. Another twelve landed at wrong fields by mistake. One broke down within Chinese territory and its crewmembers had to bale out, who were later sent to Kunming by some Chinese.

General Arnold ordered Wolfe to dispatch his B-29 bombers to air raid the territory of Japan. On June 19th, from Calcutta Airbase, India, ninety-two B-29 bombers flew to advanced airbase, Chengdu, among which one got lost on the way, landing at another field, and still other few bombers

1944 年 6 月 5 日早晨，112 架 B-29 轰炸机从印度加尔各答基地起飞，轰炸泰国曼谷的马卡桑铁路车辆工厂，这是一项往返 3220 千米的远程轰炸任务。约翰·凯勒少校机长驾驶的轰炸机，从加尔各答基地查库利亚机场起飞后坠毁，机组人员除一人外，无一生还。起飞不久，有 14 架因机械故障被迫折回。B-29 轰炸机队在 8200 米高空利用雷达瞄准具投弹进行轰炸。防空炮火很猛烈，但因高度太高打不着。只有一小批敌战斗机拦截，都被 B-29 轰炸机机上的机炮挡了回去。这是 B-29 轰炸机首次轰炸作战行动，但战果平平。

雨季刚开始，天公比敌人还作难。B-29 轰炸机进行转场训练，从印度加尔各答基地起飞，到中国昆明机场降落，飞机加油后再返回加尔各答基地。1 架起飞不久就撞在达姆达姆机场，3 架掉进孟加拉湾，12 架误降其它机场，1 架在中国境内飞机发生故障，机组人员被迫跳伞，后由中国百姓带到昆明。

阿诺德命令沃尔夫派 B-29 轰炸机空袭日本本土。6 月 19 日，92 架 B-29 轰炸机从加尔各答基地起飞，转场到成都前进基地。其中 1 架途中迷航，降落在其它机场；还有几架因故障返航，只要 79 架到达成都附近的前进基地。经检查有 68 架飞机可以执行任务。一些要人和新闻记者为了能够亲眼目睹空袭日本都挤上了飞机。飞机加油后，于下午 4 时 30 分起飞。起飞过程中，1 架 B-29 轰炸机坠毁。当晚 11 时 38 分，B-29 轰炸机在 2500 米~5500 米之间高度，用目视或雷达瞄准进行投弹。日本人已获得预警，

B-29 long-range heavy bombers of the 20th Bomber Team parking at advanced airfield, Guanghan, near Chengdu.
第 20 轰炸机队的 B-29 远程重型轰炸机，在成都附近的广汉前进基地。

Sino-American ground crew were maintaining and servicing B-29 bombers, getting them ready to perform long-distance bombing mission at any minute.
中、美两军的地勤人员在维护、保养 B-29 轰炸机，随时准备执行远程轰炸任务。

Before B-29 bombers set out, ground crew was doing maintenance.
B-29 轰炸机战斗出动前,地勤人员在进行地面维护准备。

B-29 bombers of the 20th Bomber Team were on the way to Japan to bomb the Japanese territory.
第 20 轰炸机队的 B-29 轰炸机在飞往日本,对日本本土进行轰炸。

B-29 bombers were bombing the Japanese territory and through the window, the Fuji Mountain, Japan, and another B-29 were in sight.
B-29 轰炸日本本土，透过有机玻璃弦舱可以看到日本富士山及另 1 架 B-29 轰炸机。

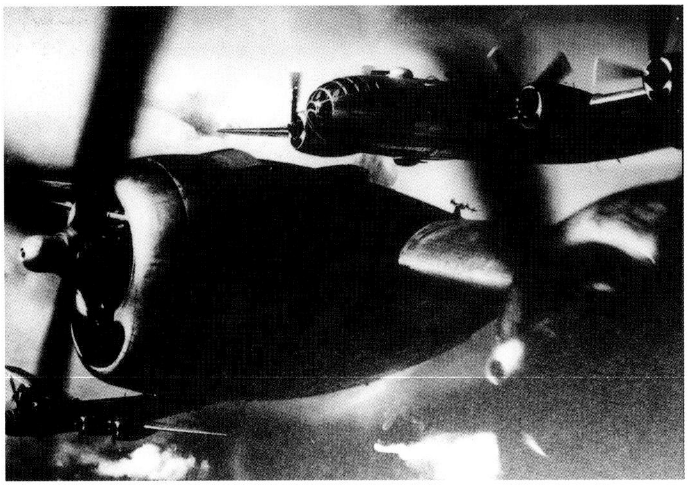

B-29 bombers of the 20th Bomber Team, from the base near Chengdu, were flying to bomb Japan. They were in a tight formation to defend each other by their own firepower, as they were lack of fighter cover.
第 20 轰炸机队的 B-29 轰炸机从成都附近基地起飞轰炸日本，由于没有战斗机护航采取密集编队，依靠轰炸机自身火力进行防卫。

B-29 bombers of the 20th Bomber Team were releasing bombs over the target area in Japan.
第 20 轰炸机队的 B-29 轰炸机在日本目标区上空投弹。

One B-29 bomber was dropping bombs in Japan while another B-29 was taking pictures above it for evaluating the bombing effects after the mission.
一架 B-29 轰炸机正在日本投弹轰炸，另一架 B-29 轰炸机在其上空照相，以便评估轰炸效果。

turned back to Calcutta because of malfunctions. At last only seventy-nine arrived at advanced airbase near Chengdu. After careful inspection, sixty-eight of the bombers could perform the bombing mission. In the interests of witnessing the air raid on Japan, some VIPs and journalists packed the bombers. After being refueled, the bombers took off at 4: 30 p.m.and unfortunately one B-29 bomber crashed during takeoff. At 11:38 that very evening, at altitude between 2,500 m and 5,500 m, B-29 bombers released bombs visually or by means of radar sight on Japanese territory. Because they were alerted in advance, the Japanese practiced blackout on Hachiman, where everything was in darkness. The bombing caused flames lighting up the sky, making the objects hard to be identified. Sixteen Japanese fighter planes fired at B-29 bombers but missed their targets. After the operation, however, one B-29 crashed on its way home with no crewmembers surviving. Another B-29 bomber was shot down by Japanese ground air-defense fire when flying over the Japanese-controlled area.

In this action, the 20th Bomber Team suffered a loss of three B-29 bombers and 30 crewmembers. The correspondents going

八幡市已实行灯火管制，灯火已全部熄灭。轰炸造成大火，使目标变得难以辨认。有 16 架日军战斗机向 B-29 轰炸机开火，但没有造成损失。轰炸结束后，1 架 B-29 轰炸机在返航途中坠毁，机上人员全部牺牲；1 架 B-29 轰炸机在返航途中通过日军控制区上空时，被地面防空炮火击中坠地。

这次作战行动，第 20 轰炸机队损失 3 架 B-29 轰炸机和 30 名机组人员。随行记者对这次空袭日本本土大事渲染。6 月 21 日，第十四航空队派侦察机到八幡市上空进行侦察，对 B-29 轰炸机轰炸效果进行评估，发现损失不大，只有发电厂厂房和市内一些工业区遭到空袭，而主要目标八幡钢铁厂基本未受到损失。

1944 年美国陆军第 20 轰炸机队从成都附近基地起飞多批 B-29 轰炸机，对日本军事基地和工业设施等目标实施大规模轰炸。主要轰炸作战行动有：

along the action played up the results of the bombing on the territory of Japan. On June 21st, the 14th Air Force dispatched a reconnaissance airplane to scout Hachiman. The evaluation of the bombing of B-29 bombers showed that the Japanese loss was not so heavy. Only a few workshops of the power plant and some industrial areas in the city suffered that air raid while the main target, Hachiman Iron and Steel Works, was not damaged on the whole.

During 1944, the 20th Bomber Team sent B-29 bombers in several batches from the airbases around Chengdu, and performed large-scale bombings on Japanese military bases, industrial establishments and other targets. The primary bombing actions were as follows:

June 15th, seventy-five B-29 bombers set off, of which forty-seven flew to Kyushu Island, Japan, dropping 400 tons of bombs on Hachiman Iron and Steel Works and other targets and leveling a number of blast furnaces and workshops to the ground.

July 7th, eighteen B-29 bombers were sent and bombed the navy bases in Sasebo and other places in Kyushu Island.

July 29th, seventy-two B-29s flew to bomb the Japanese-controlled iron and steel base in Northeast China, Anshan Iron and Steel Works, resulting in a heavy damage to most of the facilities of the works and steel output reduction by 3/4.

August 20th, sixty-one B-29 were sent to bomb the military bases, industrial establishments and other objects in Kyushu Island, Japan.

September 8th, ninety-five B-29 bombers went to bomb Japanese-controlled military and industrial targets in Anshan, Shenyang, Dalian, Benxi and other places in China, with 206 tons of bombs released.

September 24th, seventy-two B-29 bombers carried out the mission to bomb the Japanese military and industrial targets in Anshan, Shenyang, Dalian and other places, China.

November 11th, ninety-five B-29 bombers were sent out. Their original plan was to bomb the military targets at Omura in Kyushu Island, Japan. Due to the effect of typhoon, sixty-one of them changed their course, under orders, to bomb Nanjing, resulting in a heavy loss of Japanese army there. Not receiving radio signals, the others bombed the military targets of Omura in Kyushu Island as scheduled.

November 21st, 109 B-29 bombers roared again to bomb the military targets of Omura in Kyushu Island, Japan.

December 7th, ninety-one B-29 bombers were ordered to bomb the Japanese-controlled airports, railway stations and ordnance factories and other targets in Shenyang and other places.

December 21st, forty-nine B-29s air raided Japanese bases and logistic accommodation facilities in Liaoning area.

6月15日,起飞75架B-29轰炸机,其中47架飞至日本九州岛对八幡钢铁厂等目标投弹400吨,使许多高炉和厂房化为废墟。

7月7日,起飞18架B-29轰炸机,轰炸日本九州岛佐世保等海军基地。

7月29日,起飞72架B-29轰炸机,轰炸日军在中国东北的钢铁基地——鞍山钢铁厂,使大部分设施遭到严重破坏,钢产量减少3/4。

8月20日,起飞61架B-29轰炸机,轰炸日本九州岛的军事基地和工业设施等目标。

9月8日,起飞95架B-29轰炸机,轰炸日军控制的鞍山、沈阳、大连、本溪等地的军事及工业目标,投弹206吨。

9月24日,起飞72架B-29轰炸机,轰炸日军在鞍山、沈阳、大连等地的军事及工业目标。

11月11日,起飞95架B-29轰炸机,原计划轰炸日本九州岛大村的军事目标,因受台风影响,其中61架奉命改航轰炸南京,使南京的日军损失惨重。其余飞机因未收到无线电讯号,仍按计划轰炸了九州岛大村的军事目标。

11月21日,起飞109架B-29轰炸机,再次轰炸了日本九州岛大村的军事目标。

12月7日,起飞91架B-29轰炸机,轰炸日军在沈阳等地的机场、火车站及兵工厂等目标。

12月21日,起飞49架B-29轰炸机,轰炸辽宁地区的日军基地及后勤供应设施。

B-29 bombers in formation were roaring to bomb the Japanese-controlled military and industrial targets in Anshan, Shenyang, Dalian, and other places.
B-29 轰炸机编队在飞往鞍山、沈阳、大连等地，准备轰炸日军控制的军事及工业目标。

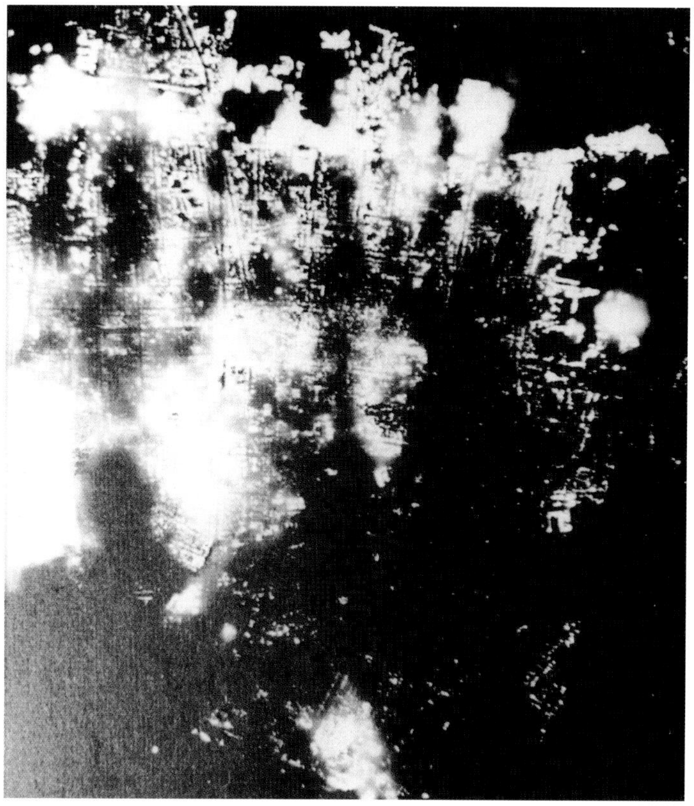

On the night of August 1st, 1945, B-29 bombers of the 20th Bomber Team dropped incendiary bombs, and hit an aluminum ware center in Toyama, Japan.
1945 年 8 月 1 日夜间，第 20 轰炸机队的 B-29 轰炸机使用燃烧弹命中日本富山的铝制品中心。

After a bombing mission, a B-29 bomber was landing on the runway at Pengshan airfield near Chengdu. We can find the runway was still uneven after a rush repair.
执行任务归来的 B-29 轰炸机在成都附近的彭山机场降落，可以看出抢修的跑道并不平整。

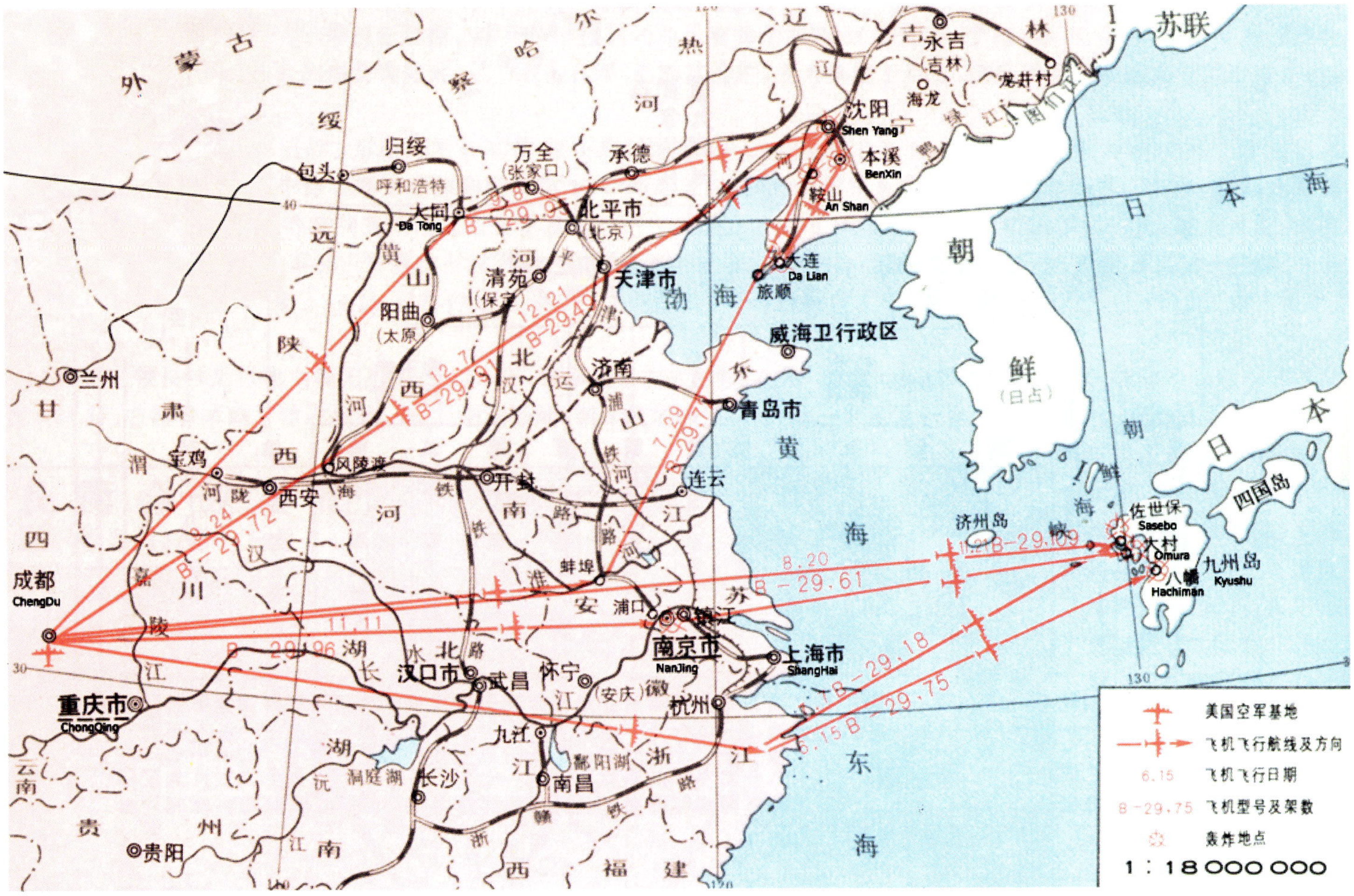

This is a sketch map of B-29 Bombers of the 20th Bomber Team bombing Japanese military bases and industrial establishments (between June and December, 1944).

美国陆军第 20 轰炸机队 B-29 轰炸机轰炸日本军事基地和工业设施示意图(1944 年 6 月至 12 月)

During the mid-June 1944, Japanese armies enhanced their attacks on the whole East China. At the same time, however, American Marine Corps landed on Saipan occupied by Japan, and they built a strip for B-29 bombers on the island as the advanced airbase for attacking Japanese territory. B-29 bombers took off from the airbases in India, flew to the airfields around Chengdu, China, for refueling, and then flew to Saipan strip. Since October 1944, the 14th Air Force expanded the advanced airfields for B-29 bombers around Chengdu, and pressed on with raising fuel and logistic materials to guarantee the service for B-29 bombers, thus ensuring B-29 bombers' strategic bombing on Japan.

1944 年 6 月中旬，日军在中国东部地区全面加强进攻。与此同时，美国海军陆战队在日本占领的塞班岛登陆，并在岛上为 B-29 轰炸机建立简易机场，作为进攻日本本土的前进基地。从印度基地起飞的 B-29 轰炸机，转场到成都周围机场加油后，再飞往塞班岛简易机场。从 1944 年 10 月起，第十四航空队对成都周围 B-29 轰炸机的前进机场又进行扩建，并加紧筹措油料和后勤保障物资，为 B-29 轰炸机对日本实施战略轰炸提供各种勤务保障。

3-5

Rescue Lt. Robert Wesselhoeft

营救罗伯特·威瑟尔霍夫特中尉

On June 27th, 1944, in order to rescue Lt. Robert Wesselhoeft, a pilot of the 14th Air Force, a report reached Yunnanyi Airbase of the 14th Air Force, saying that Lt. Robert Wesselhoeft had fallen seriously ill while carrying out his duty in Lanping, west Yunnan. Although under the tender care of the Lanping people, Lt. Robert Wesselhoeft needed emergency medical treatment, which was lacking in the small Lanping village. The American Army dispatched a small airplane from Yunnanyi Airbase to rescue him, but the 2-day attempt repeatedly failed due to overcast conditions and lack of a landing place. On June 29th, Lt. Robert Wesselhoeft's sickness became critical. The American Airbase had no choice but to dispatch a medical team to go to Lanping via precipitous land route in a jeep. After 5 days' hard journey, the team reached Lanping on July 3. By that time, the lieutenant was breathing with great difficulty, and it seemed that he was dying. It was realized that the only hope to save him would be sending him to the war hospital right away. However, it would take more than ten days to reach the American war hospital in India, or at least 5 days to drive him to the war hospital in Baoshan or in Yunnanyi. But he was in critical condition and it seemed unlikely he could stand the ordeal of the trip. The American rescue team was caught in the dilemma. Then the Lanping people came up with the suggestion of building a make-do airstrip in the spacious mountain valley for the rescue plane, which the team thought worthy of a try. To build the airstrip meant to race against time and to win time meant to save Robert's life. The local people immediately started the work despite of untold difficulties. After 3 day-and-night's hard work, they had the airstrip completed.

1944年6月27日，美国陆军第十四航空队云南驿基地接到报告，罗伯特·威瑟尔霍夫特中尉在云南西部兰坪执行任务时身患重病。兰坪民众精心照料罗伯特·威瑟尔霍夫特中尉，但是小山村缺医少药，罗伯特中尉急需救治。美军派一架小型飞机从云南驿基地前来救助，但兰坪上空乌云密布，能见度很差，连续2天找不到降落地点。6月29日，罗伯特中尉病情恶化。美国只得从基地派出医疗队乘吉普车从陆路赶往兰坪，经过5天5夜艰苦跋涉，于7月3日到达兰坪。这时，罗伯特中尉呼吸困难，生命垂危，必须及时送往美军战地医院抢救。但是，从兰坪到在印度的美军战地医院有10天的路程，到保山或云南驿战地医院至少需要5天，罗伯特虚弱的身体，已禁不住路途的颠簸和劳累。兰坪农民建议在空旷的山谷里为营救飞机修建一条临时跑道，美军医疗队认为值得一试。修建跑道意味着与时间赛跑，赢得了时间就赢得了罗伯特的生命。兰坪农民立即在艰难的条件下，经过3天3夜艰苦奋战，一条临时跑道建好了……

The American rescue team reaching Lanping via precipitous land route in a jeep to rescue Lt. Robert Wesselhoeft.
为了救治罗伯特·威瑟尔霍夫特中尉，乘吉普车从陆路赶到兰坪的美军医疗队。

In Lanping valley, the people starting to construct a make-do airstrip on the uneven hillside fields with primitive and simple tools in order to rescue Lt. Robert Wesselhoeft.
兰坪的山谷，为了救治罗伯特中尉人们用原始、简陋的工具，要在这高低不平的坡地，修建平坦的临时跑道。

Lanping's people digging stones.
兰坪农民在挖取石块

Lanping's people moving stones to construct the airstrip despite the raining.
兰坪农民冒雨搬来石块修建临时跑道。

In order to send Lt. Robert to the war hospital to be rescued, Lanping's people and the American medical team all hoped to complete the airstrip as soon as possible.
兰坪的民众和美军医疗队人员都在期盼临时跑道能够早日修好，以便将罗伯特中尉早日送到战地医院抢救。

Welsh, a pilot of the 14th Air Force in Yunnanyi airbase, piloted an L-4A "Piper" small liaison airplane to Lanping and landed it safely on the airstrip. Lt. Robert was carried into the airplane and was eventually saved.

美国陆军第十四航空队云南驿基地的威尔士驾驶L-4A“风笛手”小型联络机，在临时跑道上安全地降落，兰坪民众将罗伯特抬上飞机。罗伯特·威瑟尔霍夫特中尉终于得救了。

Welsh, the pilot, standing by the L-4A"Piper" small liaison airplane.
驾驶员威尔士在L-4A“风笛手”小型联络机旁

L-4A "Piper" liaison airplane.
L-4A“风笛手”联络机

People all running to the airstrip to welcome the coming rescue aircraft.
人们都奔向临时跑道迎接救援飞机的到来

Lanping's people carrying Lt. Robert, wading across a river, and hurrying on with their journey to the make-do airstrip.
兰坪民众抬着罗伯特中尉涉水过河，将他送到临时跑道。

Lanping's people wading across a river with the American medical team members of the rescue team on their backs, hurrying on with their way to the make-do airstrip.
兰坪民众背着美军医疗队人员涉水过河，赶往临时跑道。

Lanping's people carrying Lt. Robert into the airplane.
兰坪民众将罗伯特中尉抬上飞机

3-6

Rescue American Pilots

营救美国飞行员

During the Anti-Japanese War , the Chinese would do their utmost to help the American pilots who were fighting in China Theater, no matter which team they were from (such as A.V.G, the 23rd Fighter Group of the 10th Air Force, and the 14th Air Force) and no matter what kind of conditions they were in (such as being shot down or damaged by Japanese forces, airplane failure, being forced to bale out or being forced to land). Some of the pilots were rescued by the Eighth Route Army and the New Fourth Army. In the book *Col. C. L. Chennault*, written and edited by Mr. Jack Samson, one of the original Flying Tigers members, there are descriptions such as the New Fourth Army rescued the American pilots who were shot down in the battles in East China.

In order to make the American pilots rescued in time, China"Aviation Commission"made a special help marker which could be seen on the flight jackets or working uniforms. The American army had also made such kind of marker with Chinese, Burmese and English characters on them. At that time, those markers were called Life-saving Talisman or Xuepiao (blood written talisman).

How many American pilots were rescued by the New Fourth Army and the Eighth Route Army and what were their names of the rescued, nobody knows, because it was impossible to count the number and names exactly in the war. However, the friendship between the Chinese and American peoples established in the Anti-Japanese War reappeared in some remaining valuable documents.

在抗日战争期间，从美国志愿航空队、美国陆军第十航空队第 23 战斗机大队到美国陆军第十四航空队，在空中被日军飞机击落、击伤，或飞机发生故障，飞行员被迫跳伞或者迫降，都会得到中国人的救助。其中部分美国飞行员得到新四军、八路军的营救。原“飞虎队”成员杰克·萨姆森编写的《陈纳德》书中就有在中国华东地区作战“被打下的美国飞行员均被中国的新四军救起”的记载。

为了使美军飞行人员能够及时得到救助，中国“航空委员会”专门制作了可以缝在飞行员的飞行服或工作服上的救助标识。美军也制作了印有美国国旗和中文、英文、缅甸文等文字的求助标识。当时有人称这些标识为“救命符”、“血票”。

新四军、八路军营救的美国飞行员有多少？他们的姓名？由于战争年代受条件限制，有些资料没有保存，有些保存的资料散失了，已无法统计被营救的人数及他们的姓名。但是，找到一些幸存的珍贵史料。这些珍贵的史料，又让人们重新看到了当年中、美两国军民共同抗击日本法西斯的战斗情谊。

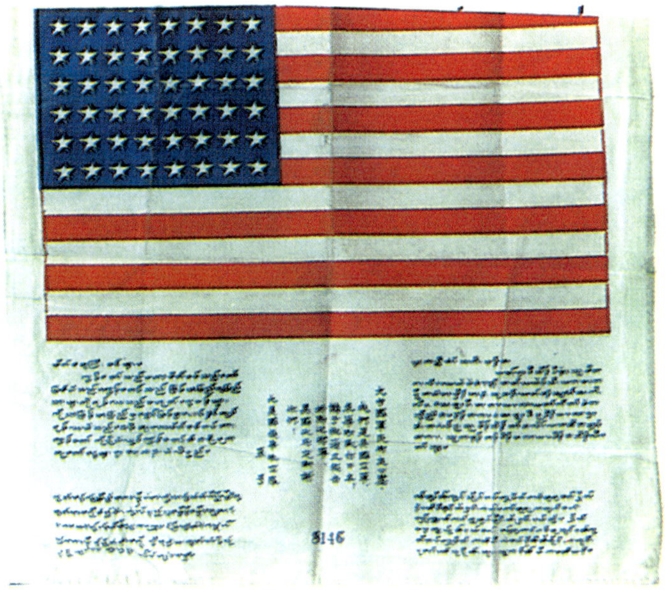

The help markers made by American, on which were the national flag of the U.S., and Chinese, Burmese and English characters that read: "All Chinese Army Men and Civilians are requested to send this American pilot, who are helping China in the fight against Japan, to a Chinese or American Garrison."
美军制作的印有中文、英文、缅甸文"我们是美国空军来华助战打日本鬼子，请把我们送到有中国军队或有美国人的地方"及美国国旗的救助标识。

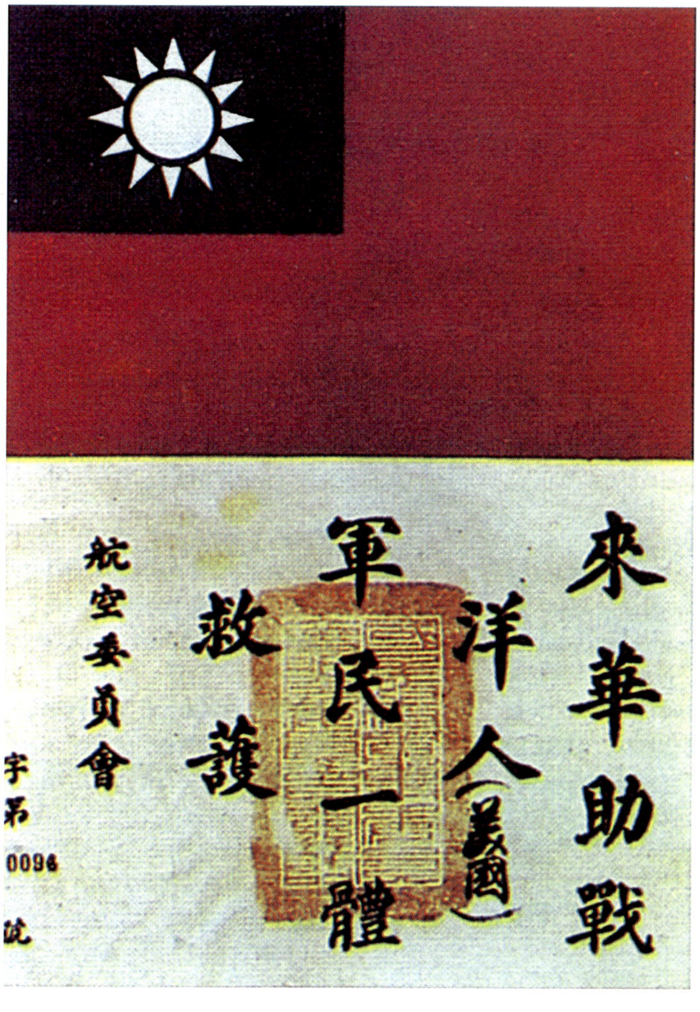

Help markers made by China's "Aviation Commission", on which are the national flag of China at that time, and Chinese characters that read "All Chinese Army Men and Civilians are requested to rescue and protect this foreign (American) pilots who is helping China in the fight".
中国"航空委员会"制作的印有中国国旗及"来华助战洋人(美国)军民一体救护"字样的救助标识。

During those years in Kunming, posters like this one could be seen everywhere in the city.
当年昆明街头随处可见营救美军飞行员的招贴画

On May 5, 1944, 10 B-24D Bombers of the 14th Air Force, covered by 20 P-51 fighters took off from the Lingling Airbase, Hunan, to make a surprise attack on the Japanese-controlled Hankou Airbase. While passing over Jianli, Hubei, one P-51 fighter, No. 7369949, was out of control due to mechanical failure, the pilot, Yerirola by name, had to bale out. Fortunately, he was rescued by the New Fourth Army stationing in this area. At the military base, although the soldiers of the New Fourth Army cooked rice and eggs for him, the rescued pilot could not get used to the food due to his dietary habits. One day, Mr. Yarirola mumbled, "sugar, sugar" while beating his enamel bowl. Xia Kui, a soldier of the New Fourth Army guessed what he wanted by his little knowledge of English. But at that time, sugar was in short supply in the base. The soldiers ran risks to buy a pound of sugar at Japanese-controlled Xingou Town. Yaririla was very overjoyed when he got the sugar. He waited no time to wash the pan, light a fire, asking Xia Kui to help add wood into the fire by gestures. After putting some boiled rice into the pan, he added two spoons of sugar into the rice and mixed them together. After a while, he put the rice into his bowl and ate it, laughing from ear to ear. Later, Mr. Yerirola was sent to the 5th Division Headquarters of the New Fourth Army at Dawushan, Hubei Province. In order to make him comfortable, he was settled at Quanshuisi (Spring Mosque which was called International Hotel by joking). The New Fourth Army prepared a new quilt and a mosquito net for him and, what was more, specially arranged a political instructor, who had once cooked some western food in Wuhan, to prepare food for him. An army man, who fought on the field, successfully cooked typical western food in a mountain village for an American friend, such as toast, roast beef, pork etc., with simple cookers, which impressed Yerirola deeply.

Later on, all the American pilots rescued in E-Yu-Wan Area (short for Hubei Province, Henan Province and Anhui Province) were sent back to America via Chongqing. Many soldiers of the New Fourth Army and the Eighth Route Army were wounded and some even gave their lives while rescuing American pilots.

1944年5月5日，第十四航空队从湖南零陵基地起飞10架B-24D轰炸机在20架P-51战斗机的掩护下，突袭日本空军汉口基地，其中1架P-51战斗机在湖北监利上空，因机械故障飞机失去操纵，飞行员被迫跳伞。飞行员落地后，被驻地新四军营救。这名飞行员叫叶里洛拉，驾驶P-51战斗机，机号为7369949。新四军为他做大米饭、炒鸡蛋。由于饮食习惯的差异，一天，叶里洛拉敲打搪瓷碗，嘴喊着“Sugar，Sugar”。略懂几句英语的新四军夏夔知道他要“糖”。根据地买不到白糖，新四军战士就化装到日军占领区的新沟镇购买了1斤白糖。叶里洛拉拿到白糖非常高兴，他把铁锅洗干净，点火做饭，比划着要夏夔帮他添材加火。他把煮熟的大米饭倒在锅里，再加上两勺白糖翻炒几下，装在搪瓷碗，笑兮兮地吃了起来。不久，叶里洛拉被转送到湖北大悟山新四军第5师师部。为了照顾美国飞行员的生活，在泉水寺为他安排了住处(戏称“国际招待所”)，准备了新被子和蚊帐；还抽调1名曾在武汉做过西餐的教导员，专门为叶里洛拉烤面包、烧牛排、猪排……一个拿枪的中国军人，在山村里用原始的锅灶、简陋的厨具，做出了地地道道的西餐，使叶里洛拉深受感动。

后来，在鄂(湖北)、豫(河南)、皖(安徽)地区被营救的美军飞行员都辗转经重庆回到美国。为了营救美军飞行员，有些新四军、八路军负了伤，有的牺牲了。

In the summer of 1944, Mr. Luo Guangda, an accredited journalist of the Ji-Re-Liao (the abbreviation for Hebei Province, Rehe Province and Liaoning Province) Military Area Command, was reviewing the American pilot rescued by the Eighth Route Army.

1944年夏天，冀(河北)、热(热河)、辽(辽宁)军区特派记者罗光达在河北昌黎采访被八路军营救的美国飞行员。

General Li Da, a commander of the China Eighth Route Army, having a picture taken with the rescued American pilots.
八路军将领李达与被八路军营救的美国飞行员合影

Yerirola, a rescued pilot of the 14th Air Force, talking with an army man of the New Fourth Army.
新四军与被营救的第十四航空队飞行员叶里洛拉交谈

Commanders and soldiers of the New Fourth Army with Yerirola, a rescued pilot of the 14th Air Force.
新四军指战员与第十四航空队飞行员叶里洛拉合影

The New Fourth Army holding a welcoming party for the rescued American pilots and having a warm-hearted talk with them.
新四军欢迎被营救的美国飞行员并与他们进行交谈

The rescued American pilots enjoying themselves.
被营救的美国飞行员在娱乐

General Li Xiannian, Commander of the New Fourth Army, having a picture taken with the rescued American pilots.
新四军领导人李先念与被营救的美国飞行员合影

General Li Xiannian, Commander of the New Fourth Army, with the rescued American pilots.
新四军的领导人李先念与被营救的美国飞行员合影

Here's where the New Fourth Army rescued American pilots used to live, Quanshuisi (Spring Mosque).
当年被新四军营救的美国飞行员住过的泉水寺旧址

In August 1944, General Zhang Aiping, the 4th Division Commander of the New Fourth Army, had a picture taken with the rescued American pilots.
1944 年 8 月，新四军第四师师长张爱萍与被营救的美国飞行员合影。

In 1984, forty years later after the American pilots were rescued by the New Fourth Army, Mr. Zhang Aiping, Chinese National Defense Minister , during visiting USA, met with these pilots alive, talking about the Sino-American militant bands of friendship made by the peoples and armies of the two countries during the war jointly against Japanese fascists.
40 年后的 1984 年，当年新四军第四师师长，时任中国国防部部长的张爱萍访问美国时，与当年被新四军营救的尚健在的美国飞行员会面，大家在一起共叙了中、美两国军民共同抗击日本法西斯的战斗情谊。

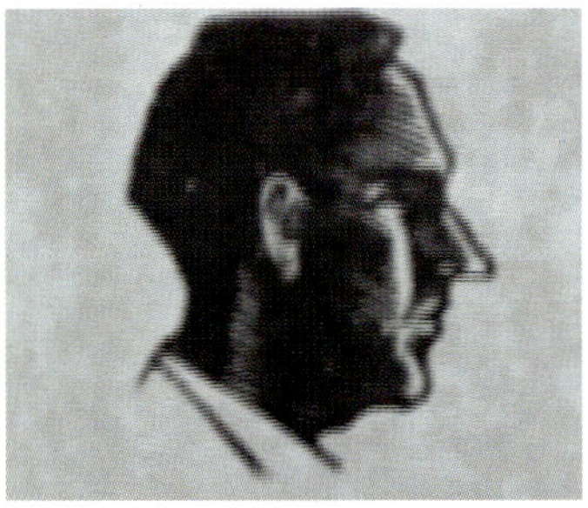

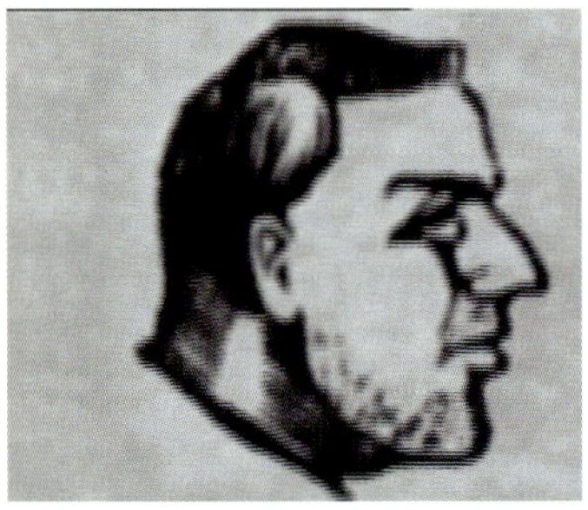

Some heads of rescued American pilots, woodcut by the artists of the New Fourth Army, due to lack of photographic equipments.
当时没有摄影条件，新四军的美术工作者采用木刻的方式，记录了部分被营救的美国飞行员的头像。

3-7

Search for Bomber No. 40783

寻找40783机组人员

On October 2, 1996, two Chinese farmers Pan Qibin and Jiang Jun in Guangxi Province, entered a virgin forest on the Mao'er Mountain, the highest in South China and a nature preserve, to collect medicinal herbs. They accidentally discovered wreckages of a crashed plane hanging on the cliffs and reported it to the local government, which repeatedly dispatched personnel to investigate the site, organized the local people to protect the crashed plane.The Chinese Foreign Ministry informed the concerned party of the United States about the discovery.

In January 1997, a searching team, composed of Sino-American experts, was set up to search for the missing crewmembers of the bomber. The Office of Missing Personnel under the U.S. Department of Defense sent to China an Experts Group headed by Vice Director Allen Leota to join related Chinese departments in the site investigations. It had been confirmed that the plane was the No. 40783 B-24D Bomber that crashed 53 years ago.

The Chinese and U. S. governments spared no efforts to search for remains of the 10 crewmembers in the virgin forest at an elevation of 2,000meters. As the incident happened ages ago and the wreckages of the bomber were scattered in a large area, the searching team met a great difficulties in collecting the remains of the missing crewmembers. They, together with others, labored themselves by primitive means to find the remains.

1996年10月2日，中国广西农民潘奇斌和蒋军进入广西猫儿山自然保护区猫儿山采药，他们在猫儿山悬崖断壁上发现了飞机残骸，并向当地政府作了报告。当地政府多次派人到飞机残骸现场勘察，并对现场采取了有效的保护。同时，将情况报告了中国有关部门。中国外交部把这一情况通报给了美国有关方面。

1997年1月，由中、美两国专家组成的搜寻小组，到广西猫儿山寻找失踪的机组人员。经美国国防部失踪人员事务办公室副主任艾兰·列奥塔率领的专家小组和中国有关部门的专家实地调查，确认这架飞机是53年前失踪的美国陆军第十四航空队机号为40783号的B-24D轰炸机。

中、美两国人员不遗余力地在海拔2000多米的原始森林中搜寻40783号飞机10名机组人员的遗骸，因为时隔久远，飞机坠落后残骸散落的范围较大，寻找机组人员遗骸的工作非常困难。在大山野林中，人们用原始、简单的工具，有时甚至用手挖土，找到了机组人员的遗骸。

On January 17, 1997, a ceremony was held at the Capital Airport in Beijing to hand over the remains of the crew of the No. 40783 Bomber to the United States. Through the Sino-American joint efforts, the missing personnel of the No. 40783 B-24D Bomber would come home for a peaceful rest.

1997年1月17日，在北京首都机场，中方代表向美方代表移交了40783号机组人员的遗骸。经过中、美两国人员的共同努力，美国陆军第十四航空队40783号B-24D轰炸机机组失踪的人员，终于可以回到自己的故乡安眠了。

The two Guangxi farmers Pan Qibin(on the left)and Jiang Jun (the right),who accidentally found the wreckages of No.40783 aircraft hanging on the cliffs.
在猫儿山悬崖断壁上发现40783号飞机残骸的广西农民潘奇斌（左）和蒋军（右）

The Mao'er Mountain with an elevation of 2142 meters, the highest in Guangxi Province.
广西最高峰海拔2142米的猫儿山

Climbing the cliffs to get to the wrekages of No.40783 aircraft.
攀登悬崖前往 40783 号飞机残骸处

The crashed engines and wing segments of B-24D on the cliffs.
坠落在悬崖上的 B-24D 轰炸机的发动机和机翼残骸

Parts of the wreckages of the control cabin of B-24D Bomber scattered on another cliff.
坠落在另一山崖上的 B-24D 轰炸机驾驶舱的部分残骸

With a pickaxe the Chinese personnel digging the remains of the crewmembers on the cliffs.
中国工作人员用手镐在山崖挖掘寻找机组人员的遗骸

With a great care, the Americans screening the bones of the crewmembers.
美方人员小心翼翼地用筛子筛选机组人员的遗骨

The Americans distinguishing and selecting the bones of the crewmembers.
美方人员在辨认、挑选机组人员的遗骨

In an accident that occurred on January 14, 1997, an American news reporter who was investigating the site of the crashed plane fell down a 60-meter-deep cliff. With the help of Pan Qibin and the local people, the American reporter was rescued successfully.
1 月 14 日，一名美国记者在飞机残骸现场采访时，不慎摔下 60 多米深的悬崖。在潘奇斌和当地群众的救助下，这位美国记者成功的脱险。

THE WHITE HOUSE

WASHINGTON

March 19, 1997

Pan Qiwen
People's Republic of China

Dear Pan Qiwen:

Thank you very much for your selfless act of heroism in rescuing Voice of America journalist Stephanie Ho after she fell at Maoer Mountain.

Your courageous efforts will be long remembered, not only by Americans and Chinese, but by people across the globe, as an example of compassion that transcends nationalities or cultural differences. You have shown yourself to be a true citizen of the world, and I commend you for your bravery and resourcefulness. On behalf of a grateful nation, please accept my most heartfelt thanks.

Sincerely,

Bill Clinton

Mr. Bill Clinton, President of the United States, wrote to Pan to show his heartfelt gratitude and appreciation.
美国总统比尔·克林顿致信潘奇斌，为他救助美国记者的英雄行为表示感谢和敬意。

This is No. 40783 B-24D Bomber of the 14th Air Force. The picture shows the plane's 10 crew in front of B-24D Bomber.
美国陆军第十四航空队机号为 40783 号的 B-24D 轰炸机，10 名机组人员生前在 B-24D 轰炸机前合影。

On January 17, 1997, a ceremony was held at the Capital Airport in Beijing to hand over the remains of the crew of the No. 40783 aircraft to the United States.
1977 年 1 月 17 日，中、美双方在北京首都机场举行了 40783 号机组人员遗骸交接仪式。

3-8

Leave China with Regret

带着遗憾离开中国战场

The Yunnan--Burma highway, an important international communication line, was cut off in May 1942 by the Japanese forces, leaving the fuel and logistic supplies to the American Volunteer Group in critical situation. According to the Lend Lease Act, war materials were airlifted to Kunming, China from India through the Hump Route, and allocated by General Stilwell. As the planned fuels, ammunition, air materials and means of substance were not always available, Colonel Claire L. Chennault often had a lot of complaints about General Stilwell. Sometimes his force was almost in the situation of stopping operation owing to lack of fuels and materials so that Colonel Claire L. Chennault had to report the conditions of the A. V. G. directly to President Roosevelt. In December 1942, American Air Task Force in China was forced to stop operation for lack of war materials. It did not restore its normal operation until the next spring.

From April 1944 on, Japan launched a campaign aiming at breaking through a continental communication line, so as to connect the Japanese forces in north-eastern China with those in Singapore. On learning the intelligence, Colonel C. L. Chennault immediately reported it to General Stilwell in Burma. Unfortunately, indulging in the plan of a counteroffensive against Burma, General Stillwell did not pay any attention to the movements of the Japanese forces on the east line. Early in April, 150,000 Japanese troops were assembled to attack Henan. Colonel C. L. Chennault asked Stilwell to increase

1942 年 5 月，滇缅公路这一重要国际交通线被日军切断后，使美国志愿航空队的油料和后勤供应非常紧张。根据“租借法案”，作战物资完全靠“驼峰航线”，从印度空运到中国昆明，但这些物资由史迪威调配。陈纳德常常因得不到计划内的油料、弹药、航材及生活物资与史迪威发生摩擦。有时陈纳德因缺乏油料及物资，部队几乎处于停飞状态，陈纳德不得不直接向罗斯福总统报告美国志愿航空队的情况。1942 年 12 月，由于油料和作战物资缺乏，美国驻华空军特遣队被迫停飞。直到第二年春天，美国驻华空军特遣队才恢复正常作战行动。

1944 年 4 月起，日本发动了打通大陆交通线的作战行动，以使从中国东北直抵新加坡的日军连成一片。陈纳德获悉这一情报后，立即报告在缅甸的史迪威，但史迪威热衷于反攻缅甸的计划，对东线日军的动向未给予重视。4 月开始，日军调集 15 万兵力进攻河南，陈纳德要求史迪威增加物资供应量，以便打击进攻河南的日军。然而史迪威却要陈纳德抽调战斗机去保卫在成都附近新建的B-29 轰炸机基地。史迪威准备用这种能载弹 9090 千克、航程达 6600 千米的 B-29 超远程重型轰炸机，从成都起飞直接去轰炸日本本土。5 月，日军集中 20 万兵力进攻湖南，陈纳德奉命用 200 架飞机保卫成都B-29 轰炸机基地，另有 150 架飞机被史迪威调去支援反攻缅甸作战，仅剩下 90 架飞

General C. L. Chennault leaving the Chinese battlefield with depressed and complicated feelings
陈纳德一脸惆怅，带着极其复杂的心情离开了中国战场。

material supplies in order to repulse the offensive Japanese forces. On the contrary, General Stilwell ordered Colonel C. L. Chennault to send some fighter planes to safeguard the newly-built B-29 bomber airbases near Chengdu. In General Stilwell's opinion, B-29, an ultra long-range heavy bomber with a carrying capacity of 9090 kg of ammunition and an air range of 6600 km, would fly directly from Chengdu to bomb the native land of Japan. In May, 200,000 Japanese troops were assembled to attack Hunan. Colonel L. Chennault was ordered to assign 200 aircraft to defend the B-29 bomber airbases near Chengdu and 150 aircraft were transferred by General Stillwell to support the counteroffensive operation in Burma. As a result only 90 aircraft remained for the east line operation. In Henan campaign, the 14th Air Force performed only 12 flight operations and in Hunan campaign 202 flight operations, repeatedly bombing the Japanese forces attacking Changsha and Hengyang. On June 26th, as the Japanese were drawing near, the 14th Air Force destroyed Hengyang Airport and transferred to Lingling Airbase. On August 8th , Hengyang was occupied by Japan. Early in September, the 6th Front Army of 130,000 Japanese forces were organized to attack Guangxi. On October 11th, the Japanese occupied Liuzhou, one of the airbases of the 14th Air Force. Thus, part of the 14th Air Force was forced to transfer to the Zhijiang in the west Hunan. On October 15th, the 14th Air Force set out from Zhijiang Airbase and made a sudden attack on the Japanese-occupied Hengyang Airfield, destroying 30 Japanese fighters and 12 bombers.

Between 12th and 16th of October, 1944, 1100 aircraft including the fighter planes taking off from the aircraft carriers of the American 3rd Fleet and B-29 bombers from the airbases in China, made successive attacks on Japanese airfields and ports in Taiwan. In this massive air operation the Japanese suffered greatly with about 500 aircraft lost, many warships damaged and some scattered. Some warships sneaked into Hong Kong for asylum, from which eight ships were sunk and eleven damaged by the 14th Air Force.

General Stilwell was Commander of China, Burma and India Theatre, with his headquarter in the jungle of Burma. He

机用于东线作战。在河南战役中，美国第十四航空队仅仅战斗出动12次；在湖南战役中，美国第十四航空队战斗出动202次，对进攻长沙、衡阳的日军多次进行轰炸、攻击。6月26日，美国第十四航空队在日军迫近的情况下，焚毁衡阳机场，转至零陵基地。8月8日，日军攻占衡阳。9月上旬，日军集中组编第六方面军，大约13万兵力进攻广西，10月11日，日军攻占美国第十四航空队的一个基地柳州，第十四航空队部分兵力被迫转移到湖南西部的芷江。10月15日，第十四航空队从芷江基地出发，突袭被日军占领的衡阳机场，炸毁日军30架战斗机、12架轰炸机。

1944年10月12日至16日，美国第3舰队的航空母舰上起飞的战斗机及从中国基地起飞的 B-29 轰炸机共1100架次，连续袭击了台湾日军各机场和港口。这次大空战日军共损失500余架飞机，许多舰船被炸毁，部分舰船四处逃散，有的潜入香港避难，被第十四航空队的轰炸机炸沉8艘、炸伤11艘。

史迪威任中、缅、印战区司令，将司令部设在缅甸丛林

trained the Chinese forces there with American equipment, preparing for a counterattack from Burma on the Japanese. Mr. Chiang Kai-shek, President of China at that time, insisted that the forces be disposed in the Chinese battlefield. They had great differences on some major military issues. Stillwell was removed from his post as Commander of China, Burma and India Theatre and went back to America on 19th October, 1944. Then China, Burma and India Theatre was redivided into two theatres, China Theatre and Burma-India Theatre. Major General Wedemeyer was appointed as Commander of China Theatre and Major General Daniel Sultan Commander of Burma-India Theatre.

In November 1944, the 14th Air Force had 17,437 soldiers, 535 fighter planes and 156 bombers, among which P-51 fighter could fly as fast as 700 km per hour, 150 km/hr faster than P-40 fighter; B-24 heavy bomber was equipped with 10 machine guns and 4000 kg. of bombs, having an air range of 4500 km. Form March 1943, when it was founded, up to May 1945, the 14th Air Force shot down or destroyed 2054 enemy planes with a loss of 500 planes of their own.

After Gen. Wedemeyer took over Commander of China Theatre, war material supplies for the 14th Air Force were increased. In December 1944, Maj. General Chennault put forward the plan of attacking the Japanese base in Hankou which had been raised six months before and had come to a deadlock as Gen. Stilwell had refused to supply fuels. Gen. Wedemeyer not only supported the plan, but also dispatched 100 ultra long- range heavy bombers from Chengdu to raid Hankou with the approval of the Pentagon. On December 18th, 77 B-29 bombers launched air raids on Hankou in seven batches, destroying the Japanese largest airbase in China . From the end of 1944 on, the 14th Air Force raided the airbases of the Japanese Air Force in Guangzhou, Nanjing, Shanghai, Hong Kong, etc. and meanwhile they bombed the Japanese supply line making the supply of the Japanese war materials greatly reduced. Therefore the Japanese ground forces began to draw back and its Air Force began to decrease its flight operations. In December 1944, the 14th Air Force shot down 241 planes and 334 planes in January 1945. Right after that, as Japan began to further reduce its Air Force dispatches, the 14th Air Force shot down only 47 enemy planes in March and met only three enemy planes in April while patrolling in the air. No other Japanese aircraft were found in the air since May 15th .

On July 31st , 1945, Major General L. Chennault was removed from his post by the Command of American Air Force for a reason of health problem. But the fact was that he was in a very good health and only suffered from a light bronchitis,

中,用美式装备训练中国部队,准备从缅甸进行反攻;蒋介石则主张将兵力用在中国战场。1944 年 10 月 19 日,史迪威被免去中、缅、印战区司令职务,调回美国。将中、缅、印战区重新划分为中国战区和缅、印战区,由魏德迈少将任中国战区司令,丹尼尔·索尔登少将任缅、印战区司令。

第十四航空队在 1944 年 11 月时,共有 17437 人,战斗机 535 架,轰炸机 156 架。其中 P-51 战斗机时速达 700 千米,时速比 P-40 战斗机快 150 千米; B-24 重型轰炸机装有 10 挺机枪、载弹 4000 千克、航程 4500 千米。第十四航空队从 1943 年 3 月成立至 1945 年 5 月,共击落、炸毁敌机 2054 架,自己损失 500 架。

魏德迈接任中国战区司令后,给第十四航空队的物资供应增加了。1944 年 12 月,陈纳德再次提出他在 6 个月前提出的袭击日军汉口基地的计划,当时因史迪威拒绝提供油料而未能实现。现在,魏德迈不仅支持陈纳德的计划,而且征得五角大楼的同意,动用成都的 100 架 B-29 超远程重型轰炸机袭击汉口。12 月 18 日,77 架 B-29 轰炸机分 7 批空袭汉口,使日本空军在中国的最大基地被摧毁。1944 年底开始,第十四航空队连续袭击广州、南京、上海、香港等地日军空军基地。同时,轰炸日军的供应线,使日军作战物资的供应量大幅度降低。这时,日军地面部队开始收缩,空军出动量也开始减少。1944 年 12 月,第十四航空队击落敌机 241 架;1945 年 1 月,击落敌机 334 架。随后,日本空军出动量急剧减少。3 月,第十四航空队仅击落敌机 47 架;4 月,第十四航空队在空中巡逻只碰到 3 架敌机。5 月 15 日后,在空中再也没有发现日军飞机了。

1945 年 7 月 31 日,陈纳德少将被美国陆军航空司令部以身体健康原因免职。其实陈纳德身体很健康,只有一点点支气管炎,但丝毫不影响他作战指挥和日常工作。8 月 1 日,陈纳德的部下、朋友及成千上万的中国人,在成都双流机场欢送陈纳德。说明陈纳德在中国很得人心,许多人都不情愿他离开中国。陈纳德经“驼峰航线”到达印度,转道欧洲回到美国。

战争结束的日子已经不远了,在反法西斯战争即将取得最后胜利的关键时刻,陈纳德被调离中国战场。陈纳德是以极不情愿的心情离开中国战场的。用陈纳德的话说,“我满怀怒火和失望离开中国”。多少令他感到欣慰的是,1937 年他以一位退休上尉的身份来到中国,在中国空军当顾问;而在 8 年后,他以美国将军的身份荣归故里。

which would never interfere with his operational command and normal work. On August 1st , General C. L. Chennault's subordinates, friends and thousands of Chinese people went to Shuangliu Airport in Chengdu to see him off, which showed that he won popular support in China and people regretted his leaving China. General C. L. Chennault got to India by way of the Hump Route. From there he returned to America via Europe.

When the war was approaching to end and the Anti-Fascist War was in the crucial moment of winning victory, General C. L. Chennault was transferred away from the Chinese battlefield. He left there, greatly depressed. General C. L. Chennault once said, "I left China with anger and disappointment." To his relief, he came to China as a retired captain in 1937 and worked as a consultant for the Chinese Air Force; eight years later , he returned to his native country with honor as a general.

Led by General C. L. Chennault, the American Volunteer Group (AVG), American Air Task Force in China and the 14th Air Force shot down and destroyed 2,500 enemy planes with a loss of 568 planes of their own during the War of Resistance against Japan. General Claire L. Chennault and his Flying Tigers , American Air Task Force in China and the 14th Air Force made great contribution to the Anti-Japanese War in China.

Mr. Kohashi, Japanese Lieutenant General and Commander of Central China Task Force, said at the end of the World War II, "60%-75% of the effective counteroffensives against the Japanese forces in China were launched by the 14th Air Force led by General C. L. Chennault. Without the 14th Air Force the Japanese forces could have advanced to anywhere they wanted to go."

Henry H Arnold, Commander-in-chief of the American Air Force, appraised General C. L. Chennault like this: he led the smallest Air Force of American Army (the 14th Air Force is the smallest one of the American Air Forces with only 600 aircraft in all, while the 8th Air Force to Britain had 8,000 aircraft at its height. Therefore, the 14th Air Force was made fun of by American pilots, calling it the Air Force on a Shoe String.). Although being beset by material supplies, the 14th Air Force destroyed many enemy naval vessels, ships, material and equipment. His force became the main factor to weaken the enemy's air offensive in the Chinese battlefield, greatly exceeding the original plan aiming at only limiting the Japanese air and ground operations. In carrying out his mission, General C. L. Chennault exhibited his tactical and strategic techniques, foresight, sagacity and military attainments, which won great honor for himself and the whole army.

陈纳德领导的美国志愿航空队、美国驻华空军特遣队和第十四航空队，在抗日战争期间，共击落、炸毁敌机2500架，自身损失568架。陈纳德及其领导的“飞虎队”、美国驻华空军特遣队和第十四航空队，在中国抗日战争中做出了巨大贡献。

日本驻华中部队司令官高桥中将在第二次世界大战结束后说：“日本在中国面临的有效反击的60%至75%是陈纳德将军的第十四航空队发动的，如果没有第十四航空队，在中国的日本军队可以为所欲为地推进到任何地方。”

美国陆军航空队总司令亨利·H·阿诺德对陈纳德的评价是：他率领了一支美军规模最小的空军部队（美国陆军第十四航空队是美国最小的航空队，总共只有600多架飞机，而驻英国的美国陆军第八航空队最多时有8000架飞机。美国飞行员戏称第十四航空队是“吊在一根鞋带上的航空队”），在物资供应困难重重的条件下，消灭了敌军大量舰艇、船舶、物资及装备。他的部队所做出的贡献，以超出原拟定的仅仅限制日军空中与地面行动的设想，成为中国战场上削弱敌空中进攻的主要因素。……在执行任务时，陈纳德将军所表现出的战术与战略技巧、远见卓识与专业造诣，为他本人以及全体军人赢得了崇高荣誉。

3-9

Commemorate Forever the American Airmen Died for the Anti-Japanese War

永远纪念为抗战牺牲的美国航空人员

The Anti-Japanese War in China was an important part of the world anti-fascist war and the battlefield in China was important part of the world anti-fascist battlefield.

Of all the forces in the Anti-Japanese War, Air Force was an important force. Since the war broke out, the air and ground crew from the United States, Germany, France, Netherlands and some other countries came to China successively to help China fight against the Japanese invaders. While the Anti-Japanese War was in the most difficult time, the former Soviet Union and the United States provided China with aircraft and equipment and also sent volunteers to China to join in the war. Yang Chengwu, the former acting chief of the general staff of the Chinese People's Liberation Army once said, "After the war entered the mid-term, the American Volunteer Group and the 14th Air Force led by Colonel C. L. Chennault, came to China. In combined operations with the Chinese Air Force, they constituted a very powerful air stronghold and recaptured the air domination which had been under the control of the enemy for a long time." In the hard days of the war, many airmen laid down their lives for the victory of the Anti-Japanese War in China and the World's Anti-Fascist War. They will be remembered forever. Their names and outstanding achievements have gone down in history. Those foreign airmen sacrificed their lives for the course against fascist aggression and for the Chinese nation, and they will be commemorated by the Chinese people forever.

中国的抗日战争是世界反法西斯战争的重要组成部分，中国的抗日战争战场也是世界反法西斯战争战场的重要组成部分。

在抗击日本侵略的各种力量中，空军是一支重要的力量。抗日战争爆发后，先后有美国、德国、法国、荷兰等国家的空、地勤人员来华帮助中国抗击日本侵略者。中国抗战处在最艰难的时候，前苏联、美国向中国提供了飞机装备援助，并派遣志愿人员来华参加抗战。原中国人民解放军代总参谋长杨成武曾经说：“抗日战争进入中期以后，由美国陈纳德将军指挥的美国志愿航空队和第十四航空队来到中国，同中国空军联合作战，构成了强大的空中堡垒，夺回了长期操于敌手的制空权。”在抗日战争的艰苦岁月中，前苏联和美国许多优秀的航空人员血洒长空，为中国的抗日战争和世界反法西斯战争的胜利献出了宝贵的生命，功垂千古，他们的业绩和英名已载入史册。在抗日战争中英勇牺牲的外国航空英烈，是为反法西斯侵略而献身的，也是为中华民族而献身的，中国人民将永远缅怀和纪念他们。

In 1945,the Chinese scouts in Yunnan laying wreaths at the memorial of Chinese and American airmen who had contributed their lives in the Anti-Japanese War.
1945 年，云南童子军向在抗日战争中英勇献身的中、美航空人员的墓地敬献花圈。

Of all the international support aeronautical organizations and airmen in China during the Anti-Japanese War, General C. L. Chennault and his Flying Tigers enjoyed the best reputation. Colonel Claire L. Chennault and his Flying Tigers, American Air Task Force in China and the 14th Air Force were highly appraised and their operations against the Japanese Air Force were vividly described in the books on the Anti-Japanese War in China. Every year in August, on the anniversary of the victory of the Anti-Japanese War, articles on General Claire L. Chennault and his Flying Tigers, American Air Task Force in China and the 14th Air Force, along with their fights against the Japanese Air Force, are carried in many newspapers and magazines. Books such as *Col. Claire L. Chennault and his Flying Tigers* by Chen Xiang Mei, *Col. Claire L. Chennault* by American Jack Samson, *American Flying Tigers* by American Dunne Schurz, etc., have been translated into Chinese and published.

抗日战争期间，国际援华航空组织及人员中，陈纳德和他的“飞虎队”名气最大。许多记录中国抗日战争的图书中，都有陈纳德和他的“飞虎队”、美国驻华空军特遣队和第十四航空队的故事，对他们打击日本法西斯空军的作战行动作了介绍并给予高度评价。在每年 8 月纪念中国抗日战争胜利的日子里，不少报刊杂志都要登载陈纳德和他的“飞虎队”、美国驻华空军特遣队和第十四航空队抗击日本空军的文章。中国还翻译出版了陈香梅著作《陈纳德与飞虎队》、美国杰克·萨姆森著作《陈纳德》、美国杜安·舒尔茨著作《美洲飞虎队》等图书。

In October 1991, 330 people from the Flying Tiger Association and The 14th Air Force Association were invited to China for a visit. Some of them were received by Vice Premier Wu Xueqian at the Great Hall of the People.
1991 年 10 月，美国“飞虎协会”和“第十四航空队协会”330 人应邀来华访问，其中部分人员在人民大会堂受到吴学谦副总理的接见。

The fighting and living experiences in China are unforgettable to the veterans of the American Volunteer Group and the 14th Air Force, who set up the Flying Tiger Association and The 14th Air Force Association and often came to China in groups to look for the places where they used to work and live. The Chinese airmen and staff members who used to fight side by side with their American counterparts also went to America to visit their battle companions and exchange sentiment of friendship. The friendship between the Chinese and American peoples has been strengthened by this kind of mutual visits.

There is an airmen cemetery near Wangjiawan, a little town at the northern foot of the Zijin Mount, Nanjing, China. Buried there were more than 3500 airmen of China, the former Soviet Union, the United States and South Korea who sacrificed their lives during the Anti-Japanese War. Among those martyrs, there are 2,200 American air crewmen.

原美国志愿航空队和第十四航空队的老战士，对在中国战斗、生活的经历难以忘怀，他们分别成立了美国“飞虎协会”和“第十四航空队协会”，并经常组团来中国寻访当年战斗、生活过的地方。曾经与美国航空人员在中国反法西斯战场并肩战斗的中国航空人员和工作人员也常去美国访问老战友，共叙旧情。这种彼此互相往来，增进了中、美两国人民的友谊。

在中国南京紫金山北麓王家湾小镇附近有一座“航空烈士公墓”，这里安葬了在中国抗日战争期间牺牲的 3500 多名中国、前苏联、美国和韩国的航空人员，其中美国牺牲的航空人员 2200 多人。

Veterans of the American Air Force paying their respect to their companions whose names were inscribed on the plates.
美国航空老战士向英名碑上的战友致敬

On May 6,1993, a ceremony for laying down the foundation of the Momument to the Air Crew Martyrs was held in the cemetery of Air Crew Martys in Nanjing,Jiangsu province. More than 100 members of the American"Hump Aviation Association"and the friends of aviation circles from Russia, Singapore and Taiwan laid down the foundation of momument.
1993 年 5 月 6 日，江苏省南京“抗日航空烈士纪念碑”奠基典礼在航空烈士公墓举行。100 多名美国“驼峰”飞行协会旅行团成员及俄罗斯、新加坡、台湾的航空界人士为纪念碑奠基。

The Anti-Japanese Aviation Martyr Mounment at the northern foot of Zijinshan mountain, Nanjing.
南京紫金山北麓的抗日航空烈士纪念碑

Raymond Neilson, painted the portraits of combat heroes of the Flying Tigers, whose heroic deeds embodied those of all the Flying Tigers' airmen.

雷蒙德·尼尔逊创作了“飞虎队”战斗英雄肖像画，他们的故事是“飞虎英雄”们的缩影。

Marion Baugh died in line of duty near Kunming, January 4, 1942. In a letter to the Chinese, Marion's mother wrote, "I gave to China a young man who knew no fear. Nor did he fail to heed the call of duty. These principles and ideals were handed down to him from generations…"

莫里森·鲍，1942 年 1 月 4 日执行任务时在昆明牺牲。莫里森的母亲在给中方的一封信中写道：“我献给中国的是一个英勇无畏的儿子，他从未辜负自己的职责。他继承发扬了我们家族世代相传的精神和理想……”

Allen Christman, a flight leader, had his plane damaged in a fight with the enemy aircraft, and bailed out. He was killed by three 1-97 Nakajimas strafing him over the rice paddies south of Rangoon, January 23, 1942. Christman was a cartoonist-assistant to Milton Caniff before he joined the A.V.G..

艾兰·克里斯特曼，飞行中队长。在 1942 年 1 月 23 日的空战中，战机被敌击伤，跳伞后在仰光南部的稻田中被 3 架日机射杀。参加美国志愿航空队前，他曾任漫画家米尔顿·凯尼夫的助手。

Thomas Cole Jr., a Golden Gloves champion from Pensacola, Florida, was killed on a reconnaissance mission over Moulmein, Burma, January 30, 1942.

托马斯·科尔，曾是佛罗里达州蓬萨克拉的高尔夫球冠军。1942 年 1 月 30 日在缅甸毛淡棉上空执行侦察飞行任务时牺牲。

John Donovan, lacking one "victory" of becoming an ace, was shot down by flak in a raid over Hanoi, May 12, 1942.
约翰·多诺万，仅差一次胜利记录就可成为空战英雄。1942 年 5 月 12 日，其战机在空袭河内时被敌炮火击落。

Max Hammer, had studied aeronautical engineering at Louisiana State University. He lost control of his airplane in a monsoon over Burma on September 22, 1941, and crashed, the first casualty of the A.V.G.
麦克斯·海莫尔，曾在路易斯安那州学过航空工程学。1941 年 9 月 22 日，在缅甸的一次季风中飞机失控坠毁。这是美国志愿航空队首次人员伤亡。

Louis Hoffman, a flight leader, engaged five enemy planes before he was shot down over Rangoon on January 26, 1942. He was 44 years old, the oldest pilot flying with the A.V.G. and one of the best.
路易斯·霍夫曼，飞行中队长。1942 年 1 月 26 日，在仰光空战中与 5 架敌机拼杀，后被击落牺牲，时年 44 岁。他是美国志愿航空队年龄最大、也是最优秀的飞行员之一。

Thomas Jones left his 20-year-old bride, an expectant mother, to join the A.V.G. He was killed in a fight over Kunming on May 16, 1942.
托马斯·琼斯，离别 20 岁、身怀六甲的爱妻参加了美国志愿航空队。1942 年 5 月 16 日，在昆明上空的一次战斗中牺牲。

Robert Litte shot down 10 enemy fighters and bombers before he was shot down over the Salween River.
罗伯特·里特，1942 年 5 月 22 日在萨尔温江上空被击落而牺牲，此前他共击落了 10 架敌机。

Neil Martin engaged the enemy over Rangoon on December 23, 1941. The fire from several enemy bombers converged on him, and he was shot down and killed, the first American Volunteer to die in combat over Burma.
尼尔·马丁，1941 年 12 月 23 日在仰光上空与敌机交战时，遭数架敌机围攻，被击落而牺牲。他是在缅甸空域牺牲的第一位美国志愿航空队飞行员。

Robert Sandell, who shot down 5 enemy planes in two days, was killed on February 7, 1942.
罗伯特·桑德尔，创下了两天击落 5 架敌机的纪录，1942 年 2 月 7 日牺牲。

Frank Schiel Jr. destroyed seven enemy planes before being shot down in China, December 22, 1943.
弗兰克·席尔，1943 年 12 月 22 日在中国被击落，牺牲前共击落敌机 7 架。

Frank Swartz died in a British hospital "under the combat skies of Poona".
弗兰克·史华兹,在印度浦那的空战中受伤,后在一家英国医院中身亡。

John Newkrik had 12 confirmed victories. He was killed on March 24, 1942.
约翰·纽克里克,有 12 次空战胜利纪录,1942 年 3 月 24 日牺牲。

John Petach Jr. married Emma Foster, an army nurse attached to the A.V.G. He was killed on July 10, 1942. A daughter was born to Mrs. Petach on February 17, 1943.
约翰·彼泰克,与美国志愿航空队女护士爱玛·福斯特结婚,1942 年 7 月 10 日牺牲。1943 年 2 月 17 日,女儿出生。

Ben Foshee, a wing man, died on May 4, 1942 of wounds received during an enemy bombing raid near Baoshan in western Yunnan Province.
本·福什,僚机飞行员。1942 年 5 月 4 日敌机轰炸滇西保山时受伤,后不治身亡。

Henry Gilbert, a former Navy dive-bomber and patrol pilot, was shot down in aerial combat over Rangoon, December 23, 1941.
亨利·吉尔伯特，曾为海军轰炸/巡逻机飞行员。1941 年 12 月 23 日，在仰光上空的空战中被击落而牺牲。

Lacy Mangleburg, a Georgian, was killed on December 23, 1941 in a training flight.
莱西·蒙格尔伯格，乔治亚州人，1941 年 12 月 23 日在一次飞行训练中遇难。

In March,1993, ten pilots of US Flying Tigers,still alive, got together in Washington. In order to accumulate the money for extending the Shanghai Tongren Hospital,they were to auction 600 copies of oil painting"Air Encounter Over Guilin", which described their air battle against Japanese Air Forsce in WW Ⅱ. Ms. Chen Xiangmei,Gen.C.L.Chennault's wife, initiated this activity. Here shows the pilots added their signatures to the duplicates.

美国“飞虎队”尚健在的 10 名飞行员，1993 年 3 月在华盛顿聚会，共同为即将拍卖的 600 幅描绘二次大战时他们在广西同日本空军作战的油画《桂林上空遭遇战》复制品签名，为扩建上海同仁医院筹款。曾率领“飞虎队”在中国抗击日军的陈纳德将军的夫人陈香梅女士发起这次活动。

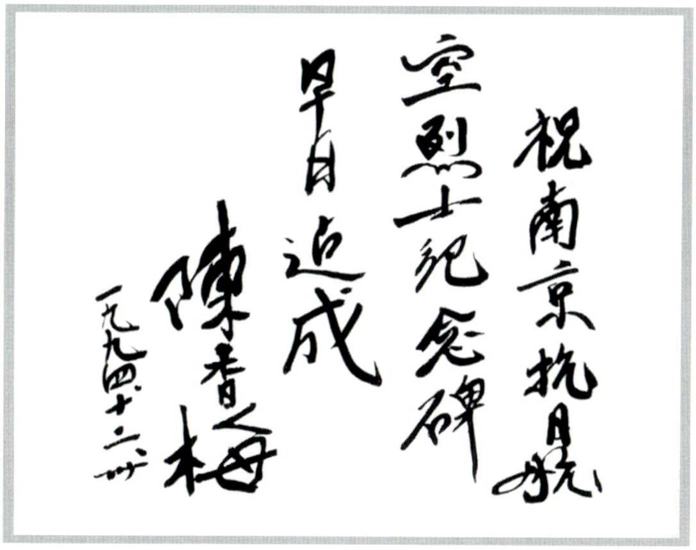

On December 30th 1994, Ms. Chen Xiangmei, General Claire L. Chennault's wife, writing an inscription for the Monument to the Air Crew Martyrs in the Anti-Japanese War.

1994 年 12 月 30 日，陈纳德将军的夫人陈香梅女士为抗日航空烈士纪念碑题词。

In Nov.1999,US-Sino Aviation History heritage Foundation in Los Angeles Aeronautic Museum performed ceremony to mourn the American Flying Tigers pilots who devoted their lives in helping China against Japanes aggressors in WW Ⅱ. Seven veterant pilots of Flying Tigers invited in the ceremony told the story about their fighting together with Chinese People and how the Chinese farmers ran the risk rescuing the US pilots.

1999 年 11 月，美中航历史遗产基金会在美国洛杉矶飞行博物馆举行仪式，悼念在第二次世界大战中为帮助中国抵抗日本侵略军而牺牲的美国“飞虎队”将士。当年“飞虎队”的 7 位老飞行员应邀在纪念仪式上讲述了自己同中国军队和人民在第二次世界大战中并肩作战，以及中国农民冒着生命危险援救美国飞行员的故事。

From Oct.17 to Nov.5,2002, a grand exhibition "the Memory of History", sponsored by the State Council Information Office of PRC, was held in Washington D.C.,Houston and other American cities, bringing the cooperation history of the two countries to life and vividly telling the stories about the intimate friendship between the Sino-American peoples and armies in the joint anti-fascist battles during the WW II by means of these more than 700 photos and over 50 valuable material objects. The exhibition consisted of "Hump Flights","Col.C.L. Chennault and the American Volunteer Group", "Rescue of the Doolittle Team" and so on, which drew attention of a lot of American veterans and media. The purpose of this exhibition was to review the history, pay tributes to those, who made great contributions to the anti-fascist war together with their families, and what is more, make the younger generation know this period of history and remember it for ever, thus promoting the friendship between the Chinese people and the American people.

2002年10月17日至11月5日，中国国务院新闻办公室在美国华盛顿和休斯顿等地举行了“历史的记忆”大型展览，以700多张图片和50多件珍贵实物，再现“二战”期间中美在反法西斯战争中的合作历史，讲述中美两国军民血肉情谊的故事。展览包括“驼峰航线”、“陈纳德和美国志愿航空队”、“营救杜利特尔轰炸机队”等内容，引起了许多美国老兵和媒体的关注。中国举办这次展览，就是为了重温历史，是为了向在反法西斯战争中作出英勇贡献的美国老兵和他们的亲属致敬，也是为了让青年一代了解这段历史，记住这段历史，以增进中美两国人民之间的友谊。

Senator Ted Stevens, Ms. Chen Xiangmei and others visiting the exhibition "the Memory of History" and taking part in the exchanging activities.

史蒂文斯、陈香梅女士等参观“历史的记忆”展览，并参加相关交流活动。

On Oct.17,2002,Dong Xilin(on left),whose father once rescued Lt. Mooney, an American pilot,met Lt. Mooney's sister, Ena L. Davis, in the Exhibition "The Memory of History" in Washington. Dong Jiyuan,Dong Xilin's father, was a well-known doctor in Yunnan province.

2002年10月17日，曾救治过美国飞行员莫尼中尉的云南名医董济元的儿子董锡林(左)，在美国首都华盛顿举行的“历史的记忆”展览会上与莫尼中尉的妹妹埃娜·L·戴维斯相见。

Ms. Chen Xiangmei, Gen. Chennault's wife, took a group picture with Yang Jiechi,the Chinese Ambassador in the USA and Senator Ted Stevens and his wife in the exhibition "the Memory of History".
陈纳德将军夫人陈香梅女士与参加“历史的记忆”展览会活动的中国驻美大使杨洁篪(左一)、美国参议院临时议长史蒂文斯夫妇(右)合影留念

On Oct.18,2002, Gen. Song Chengzhi (on left) and Gen. Li Laizhu(in middle)from China,paid their respect to the tombstone of Gen. C.L.Chennault,commander of Flying Tigers, in the Arlington National Cemetery,Washington. Sino-US veterans, attending in the exhibition"The Memory of History", held memorial activities in the Arlington National Cemetery.
2002 年 10 月 18 日,中国原炮兵司令员宋承志将军(左一)、原北京军区司令员李来柱将军(中)在美国首都华盛顿阿灵顿国家公墓瞻仰陈纳德将军的墓碑,并与前来参加“历史的记忆”展览的中美老兵在阿灵顿国家公墓举行了悼念活动。

图书在版编目（CIP）数据

陈纳德和飞虎队/马毓福著. ——北京：五洲传播出版社，2003.9
ISBN 7-5085-0285-X
Ⅰ. 陈… Ⅱ. 马… Ⅲ. ①抗日战争—中美关系—史料—图集 Ⅳ. K265.06-64

中国版本图书馆 CIP 数据核字（2003）第 080866 号

Col. C.L. Chennault and Flying Tigers

陈纳德和飞虎队

五洲传播出版社
地址：中国北京北三环中路 31 号 邮编：100088 电话：(86) 10 82008174

开本：230mm×295mm 1/16 印张：9.375
2003 年 9 月第一版 第一次印刷 印数：1-5000 册
ISBN 7-5085-0285-X/K· 459
定价：170.00 元